THE STO
LEAD MINING FAMILY

The Thompsons of
The Bell, Newbiggin, Teesdale

Norma L Smith

Dedicated to my mother,
born Hilda Thompson, 10th June 1914

Acknowledgements

June Thompson, 147 Hotham Street, Balaclava, Victoria, Australia 3183, a descendent of William Thompson (1846-1935) compiled the early part of the family history from which I worked. She used records of births, baptisms and marriages supplied by Mrs L Willis, Genealogist, of Durham. She distributed only a summary selected from the considerable amount of information that she holds, including County records, copies of wills etc.

I am very grateful for the help given to me by Dr W F Heyes who, with great thoroughness, read my text, highlighted my errors and encouraged me to publish this book.

Contents

Introduction

Last year I wrote a short history of the Thompson family who lived in both Teesdale and Weardale, which included information about the much better known Readshaw family, whom I am pleased to say are related to my mother's branch of the Thompsons. I sent a copy to Dr W F Heyes of High Dyke House, Middleton-in-Teesdale, who is a well-known local lead-mining historian and he encouraged me to have it published as a record of not only the history of local families, but of the lead mining industry in the area. I have re-written the story since then and Dr Heyes was able to recommended a publisher for me, Judith Mashiter, of Mosaic (Teesdale) Ltd, who, coincidentally, just happens to live up the road from him and his wife, in Snaisgill.

My mother, Hilda Thompson, was very proud of her forebears, particularly those on her father's side and, since her death in 1996 I have found out a lot more about the family and their history which I have added to her recollections. Some years before she died we had a visit from June Thompson, a descendent of our Teesdale Thompsons, who was born and bred in Australia, where she still lives. She talked to us about The Bell and my mother's immediate response was "Oh! The Thompsons of The Bell." Hence the sub-title of my book. As a consequence of this visit, June Thompson sent me a copy of the family tree that she had had researched. Since then she has sent me more material, which enabled me to put together a reasonable history of this local family, who lived the same lives and suffered the same hardships as their neighbours for many generations.

A holiday visit to Middleton-in-Teesdale during the war put me in touch with some of the Teesdale Thompsons, and their descendents, including Greta Watson, who lived at the mill, in Middleton-in-Teesdale. My mother's grandmother was a Collinson before she married and one of my teachers at Alderman Leach School, in Darlington, was a Miss Collinson, the daughter of the Station Master in Middleton, so I always felt an affinity with the town and the surrounding countryside in beautiful Teesdale. Add to this background my interest in genealogy, social history and writing and you will understand why I wrote this book. These people lived a hard life and, although stories like theirs have been told many times before, I find it fascinating to have known the last generations of my mother's family involved in the lead mining industry in both Teesdale and Weardale. Added to my mother's recollections I also experienced life in a dales farmhouse for a short while more than sixty years ago, before things changed, forever, which has left me with sharp mental images of the place itself and the relations I stayed with.

As it turned out, the Thompson family history in the dale went back further than I expected, but not that far back, so they too had to have had some place of origin, before they came into the Dales. Surnames can often, with a bit of research, give us one or two clues to our genetic background and the romance attached to having a surname associated with the Border Reivers was too good to miss, hence my research into the Border Country.

One of my main reasons for writing up family histories is to record, forever, the local family history, and its continuity, which is often very interesting. County Archives at Durham are always pleased to accept copies of local books. I usually send two: one for the archives and one for their library. Durham County Library Services are grateful to have copies donated for their reference shelves in public libraries. Local History Groups and Family History Groups are also pleased to have copies for their records and so it goes.

Norma L Smith
Grey Walls
Patterdale
Cumbria

The Bell, Newbiggin, 1925

The Border Reivers

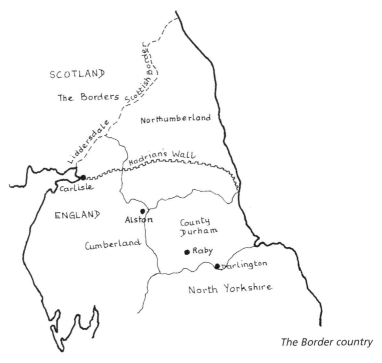

The Border country

When Henry II reclaimed Northumberland and Cumberland from the Scots in the middle of the 12th century it did not bring an end to the Border troubles, and for centuries after, disturbed political conditions over a wide band of country along the Borders brought such a high level of disruption to the way of life of the local populous that it arrested agricultural development and discouraged an increase in population. Repeatedly devastated, the Border counties remained miserable and backward. Such havoc was wrought, not only by the organised invasions of Scottish armies, but also by the Border inhabitants themselves. There was barely enough land to sustain these families. They could only recover from devastating raids by forming large clan groups that regarded the theft of cattle, sheep, goats, pigs and household goods from rival clans as the only way to survive. The levy of blackmail and the abduction of men and women from their homes to be held to ransom were common incidents of life until the end of Queen Elizabeth's reign in 1603. The more important of these people lived in fortified tower houses called 'bastles' and 'peles' but most lived in simple, clay houses, of the crofter type that clustered around the fortified house, or tower, for protection, but which were easily destroyed by raiders. Lawless, raiding clans or 'graynes' of families, living both north and south of the border between England and Scotland became known as the Border Reivers.

Who were the people who inhabited this remote Border region and where did they come from, originally? Their antecedents could have been Celts, Irish-Norse, Picts, Scots, Gauls, Anglo-Saxons, or any mixture of them all. Although the Border area has always been sparsely populated, many people passed that way and they left behind them a distinct ethnically mixed population who, in all the centuries they, and their descendents, occupied the region, seldom knew peace. During the raids south, the Scots took back home with them not only cattle and sheep, but slaves, and it is said that many Scots had English wives. Therefore, a man's loyalties to his own country could well, over the generations, have become quite blurred and may have meant less to him than loyalty to his near neighbours, whatever their nationality or origins.

By the time of the Border Reivers there were Thomsons living in Upper Liddersdale, which was the tough end of the frontier and home to its most predatory clans. The Nicksouns, or Nixons, were known as a troublesome breed and an important part of the Armstrong-Elliot-Nixon-Croser Border Reiver confederacy. Although a smaller and less compact family than the Armstrongs, they were important enough to have Thomsons, Glendennings and Hunters living under them, which is another way of saying associated with them. The Thomsons earned their keep by fighting side by side with their protectors. Liddersdale was technically part of the Scottish Middle March, but it was linked geographically and traditionally to the Western March. From Liddersdale were mounted the most devastating raids, usually into the English Middle March, where, according to Elizabethan records, a small group of Thompsons were living.

There have long been many Davidsons, Andersons, Williamsons, Robsons and Thomsons / Thompsons in the Border country. If any of these names were to form a 'clan society' it could only do so on the basis of a shared surname and not because every member was descended from one and the same original source. Sons of David, Anders, William, Rob, Robert and Thomas can emerge in areas far apart at roughly the same time and can't claim that they are all, ultimately, descended from the same ancestor. Lack of parish records and farm papers in the 16th century meant that few such country people had anything like a recorded family history. In an atmosphere of potential, or actual, violence the surname, with its 'headman' or principal, kinship structure was remarkably similar to the Highland Clan. It was localised by the acquisition of land and, in some districts, partly bounded by the wild, waste countryside.

On the western side of the country the Romans built Hadrian's Wall further south than the northernmost part of the ancient Kingdom of Strathclyde, which included Cumberland, the land of the 'Cymry'. This part of the country was home to the Celtic warriors, or Britons, who called one another 'Combrogi' meaning 'fellow countryman'. They were only partly subdued by the Romans and, as long as they didn't cause too much trouble, they were allowed to rule their own territory. Hadrian's Wall was finally abandoned in AD383, after an attack by the Picts. Three hundred years after the departure of the Romans the Celts, or Britons, were still the main tribe in the area. In AD684 when Carlisle, together with the surrounding countryside over a radius of fifteen miles, was given to Saint Cuthbert by King Ecgfrith, the once proud Celtic warriors and their families were included in the deal.

The Vikings had successfully harried the coastal area of Cumberland and the Solway for many years and, eventually, in the 9th and 10th centuries a colony of Norse-Irish spread out from north of the Solway and extended into what were to become the counties of Kirkcudbrightshire, Peebleshire and Cumberland. The settlers went inland as far as the main watershed between east and west where, today, in the lower part of the valley of Liddersdale, the border between North West England and Scotland meanders a little as the road follows the course of Liddel Water before continuing up the north side of the dale and on, across the barren hills, to the Scottish Border town of Hawick. The border itself follows a more easterly route over the Cheviot Hills to Coldstream and Berwick-upon-Tweed. Liddersdale, which lies between the two, takes its name from the early Scandinavian settlers. Dahl (dale) is a place name of Norse origin as are Haggback, Hethersgill and Scaleby, all later place names.

The Vikings didn't come and go; they stayed. One family, at least, was known to be Scandinavian and their descendents are still around. The Hetheringtons (Hetherings or Hoderings) were a Norse family who took their name from Hoedre, a Viking chief. They lived on the English side of the border and were associated with Hethersgill, north west of Brampton, where there is an old house with thick walls known as the High Gate, as well as the possible remains of a stone fortified house, or tower. They weren't active raiders but they were no better than their neighbours, being mentioned frequently in cases of both receiving and paying blackmail. They were deeply involved in a plot to murder the Bishop of Carlisle in 1569. My son's wife's family are Cumbrian Hetheringtons and their Viking origins are still apparent in their natural blonde hair colouring.

It is thought that the termination 'son' as in Thomson / Thompson is a mark of Scandinavian origin. A Cumberland deed of 1397 mentions Richard Thomson, son of Thomas Johanson, showing the use, in England, of the true Scandinavian patronymic. Thus it was that the Scandinavians added their contribution to the gene pool that was, eventually, to produce the fighting men of the Borders who, apart from farming their land, building their homes, marrying and raising their families, made history by becoming fiercely independent and warlike, taking part over the centuries in what we, today, would recognise as gang warfare and organised crime.

The Beginning of the End for the Border Reivers

The Scots raided Cumberland in 1092, 1138 and 1216, but the great part of Border raids did not begin until after the death of Edward I in 1397. The English monarchs were quite happy to leave this situation of lawlessness in the Border country as it was, forming as it did a no-man's land between England and Scotland but, by the 16th century the Earl of Moray, the leader of the Scottish Protestant nobles who were supported by Queen Elizabeth I of England against Mary, Queen of Scots, was finding the Scottish Borders a handful. Throughout 1569, especially in the Western Marches the 'innumerabil slauchteris, fyre raisinis, herschipps and detestibil enormities' by the people of Liddersdale were so bad that the inhabitants of the Scottish East and Middle Marches, in a memorandum to the Privy Council, declared themselves enemies 'to all thieves of Liddersdale, Annandale, Ewsdale, Eskdale and especially all the Armstrongs, Elliots, Nixons, Crosers, Littles, Batesons, Thomsons, Irvines, Bells, Johnstones, Glendennings, Routledges, Hendersons and Scotts of Ewesdale'.

The border soon seemed to be under control except for Liddersdale and so, in October, Moray was back and he put such fear into the inhabitants that, for the time being, 'their wes sic obedience – as the lyk wes never done to na king in na mans dayes befoir'. About one hundred Armstrongs, Johnstones, Elliots and Grahams gave pledges. These were recorded in vast numbers at Hawick on 20th October 1569. They included pledges by various people for their kinsmen and even for their whole tribe. Some were simply to be of good behaviour, but many agreed to enter themselves to be warded, until such time as 'good order could be taken with them.' In the meantime they were warded at their own expense. However, they still continued with their usual way of life, raiding and riding again harder than ever. Strife, raiding, burning and murder, it seems, were commonplace when this was a fierce and bloody frontier and were in fact the daily business of the people of the Border Country.

In 1603 a Border Proclamation was made. Sir William Seton was one of the knights named at the beginning of this proclamation and Sir Robert

Seton was named at the end.

In the agreement all people inhabiting within Tindale and Riddsdale
in Northumberland, Bewcastle Dale, Wilgavey, the north part of
Gilsland, Esk and Leven in Cumberland, East and West Tevidale,
Liddesdale, Eskdale, Ewsdale & Annerdale in Scotland (saving broken
clans) and their household servants dwelling within those several places
before recited, shall put away all armor and weapons, as well offensive
as defensive, as jacks, spears, lances, swords, daggers, steelcaps,
hagbuts, pistols, plate sleeves and such like and shall not keep any
horse, gelding or mare above the price of 50s sterling, or 30l Scots upon
the like pain of imprisonment. It is agreed that if any Englishman
steal in Scotland or any Scot steal in England any goods or cattels
amounting to the value of 12d he shall be punished by death.

Thus the inhabitants of Liddersdale were dispersed, often quite brutally. They were dispossessed of their lands and their homes destroyed. Not all of Liddersdale, where some of the Thomsons came from, was hard country. It opened out in the south where it was Armstrong territory. It is also fair to say that not all people living there were wild Reivers. The good as well as the bad, the victims and the aggressors were evicted from their homelands and they spread out into Northern England, Scotland and as far away as America. Many more were transported to Ireland and when the name occurs there, it is generally thought that **Thomson** denotes a Scottish background and **Thompson** an English background, although, whilst the families lived in the Borders, they offered no reliable allegiance to either side. The dispossessed Reivers wouldn't have had any problems finding the northern English dales as they had marauded the area quite frequently. One particular raid was recorded in 1569 when Mosstroopers, or cattle thieves, attacked the local residents of Rookhope, near Stanhope, in Weardale, taking away all their cattle and sheep.

We soon find Thomsons and Thompsons in Weardale and Teesdale, and early registers for Stanhope show a John Thompson, son of John Thompson, being baptised on 8th September 1611. Early recorded marriages include that of Elyzabeth Tomson who married Robert Stowt (Stout) on 10th

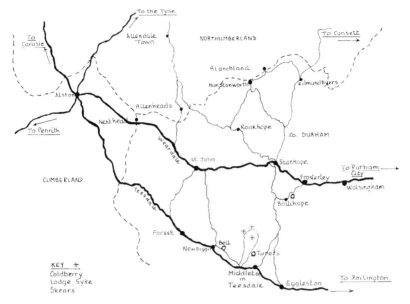

The North Pennines

November 1614. There were, and still are, many Thompsons to be found in Northumberland, where more honest employment than reiving was being provided by the industrial exploitation of that area. Despite all the setbacks these people encountered, the Thomsons and Thompsons went forth and multiplied and are now numerous in the north. There is a common saying in Scotland that 'We're all Jock Tamson's bairns.' It is used to denote people who are 'all in the same boat' or all in the same position. Many other Border names can be found in my family tree including Armstrong, Anderson, Hetherington, Bell and Scott. On the other side of the law during the Border feuds we find Whartons and my own family name of Seton (Seaton).

Thompsons in Teesdale and Weardale

First Generation

Like many people in Teesdale and beyond, my mother's line of descent from the Thompsons can be traced back to John Thompson, of Moor Rigg, Teesdale Forest, or 'Ye Forest' who married Elizabeth Bedell, also of Moor Rigg, at Middleton-in-Teesdale on 4th June 1663. There is still a farmhouse at Moor Rigg called Thompson House, which, by 1920 had fourteen acres of land, so we can, perhaps, guess that this first Thompson in the dale was a farmer. On the farm track up to Thompson House, stand Thompson Cottages. The name Bedell had even more variations in spelling in the Middleton-in-Teesdale church registers than Thompson, including the spelling Beadle, which we now accept as a local name.

Thompson House, Moor Rigg

'Ye Forest' as it was known, was the name given to dispersed settlements in Upper Teesdale within the ancient forest, which originated as a hunting area. It was not necessarily heavily wooded and it was more likely to have had a few trees, possibly birch and a covering of scrub, but as late as 1673 it was reported that four hundred deer perished there during severe weather. By 1391-2 there were shielings, or 'summer pastures' and agistments in 'Ye Forest' where farmers from lower down the dale were allowed to take their stock for summer pasture, for a fee, but by the 15th century these were being replaced by farmsteads. Much later, by 1580, many of these had become known by name. The Forest of Teesdale was divided into three parts, the South, Middle and East, the latter having sixteen tenants in 1629. In Newbiggin there were twenty-five leaseholders. Sir Henry Vane purchased the estate in 1632 and it is still in the possession of the Vane family, or Lord Barnard of Raby Castle, today; their many farmhouses, which later had their outer walls whitewashed, stand out distinctively against the green of the valley fields and the hillsides, almost from Darlington to the upper reaches of Teesdale. In 1670 there were nineteen freeholders in Middleton, twelve in Newbiggin and one or two in 'Ye Forest'. The population of the Parish of Middleton in 1660 was about 630.

The valley bottoms were cleared and stonewalls were built to enclose both the fields and the open moorland. Sheep farming was already well established in England and in 1500 there were said to be three sheep to every human being. The population then was only about two and a half to three million people, but it was slowly increasing and these people needed to be fed. Agricultural methods were improving and once the moors were drained then sheep could be kept on them, as well as stock. Those men who had security of tenure and whose families could provide the labour had a promising future.

There is a good chance that this first generation John Thompson of Moor Rigg came originally from Weardale, as his was the first Thompson marriage (4th June 1663) recorded in the Middleton-in-Teesdale parish register since marriage records began there in 1621, that is 42 years earlier, and the family obviously had stronger connections in the Stanhope area. The first marriage recorded there with a spelling of Thompson is an entry for a Thomas Thompson/Anne Watson on 22nd October 1622, with the next being Thomas Thompson/Ann Emerson, 27th November 1666, and Mary Thompson/John Emerson, 20th May 1668. Together with the first entry for Thompsons in Teesdale parish records (1663) it appears that the name was rare in these areas at the time and, as it was not then recorded as an old established local name, we can assume that the Thompsons may well have been new to the area. As not all people at that time were literate, and not all parsons careful recorders, there were often many different spellings for the same name in parish records and they can't always be relied on as being accurate, especially those from the 17th century. In Middleton-in-Teesdale registers there are Tompsons, Thomsons and Thompsons. There seem to be many more families using the spelling Thomson, but both spellings can be traced back, either in England or Scotland, to the 14th century. John was by far the most popular name for men in the family, the oldest son often being called after his father. Matthew was also a family name and a Matthew Thompson married Hannah Dixon on 30th April 1747. He may have been the brother of our third generation John, who was married in Stanhope in the previous year. The architect of the 1858 Workhouse in Stanhope was a Matthew Thompson. Romantic as it is to think that my 17th century forebears moved, or were forcibly moved, directly from the Border country to Weardale, we must consider the fact that our first John may have moved into the Stanhope area from another part of County Durham, rather than the Lowlands of Scotland. Assuming also that Matthew was a traditional family name, then only two Johns with Matthew attached and living in the same family and area are listed between 1540 and 1663 - the date of our first John's marriage:

John married in 1580 at St Nicholas Church, Durham
Matthew married in 1603 at Darlington, Co. Durham
Matthew married in 1634 at St Nicholas Church, Durham
John married in 1640 at Darlington, Co. Durham

Second Generation

It comes as no surprise that one of the second generation of Thompsons at Moor Rigg was given the name of John when he was baptised on 14th July 1672. He married Margaret Longstaff of 'Ye Forest' on 16th June 1717. The Longstaffs were fairly new to Teesdale at that time. It was during the life of this John Thompson that land on the hill above Newbiggin was purchased by the Thompson family on which they built a farmhouse, called The Bell, with two attached cottages, a cobbled farm yard and farm buildings. The datestone above the farmhouse door reads '1719 T, R and M'. There seems

The lintel stone, showing T, R M 1719

to be no record of Teesdale family members with the initials R &M, but a Robert, albeit a Thomson without a 'p', fathered a son by the name of John in Stanhope in 1636, so it could be, with different generations of the family moving between the two dales, as they did, that there were other members or branches of the Thompson family involved at The Bell, apart from those of my family line.

Third Generation

John Thompson, baptised on 14th April 1718 was the son of the above John and Margaret Thompson. He returned to Stanhope, from Teesdale, for his marriage to Anne Proud on 8th May 1746, and the death of a John Thompson of Weardale at the age of 65 is recorded in the Middleton-in-Teesdale registers on 30th March 1783.

Fourth Generation

It was at Stanhope that this fourth generation John, son of John Thompson and Anne Proud was baptised on 17th February 1754. He was referred to as a 'gentleman' from Stanhope, a term that could be used to describe a 'yeoman' farmer, in other words, someone who owned land, but he was also described as a lead miner living at Middle Side, Middleton-in-Teesdale at the time of his marriage, the Banns of which were read in Middleton church on 16th April 1786. His marriage, however, took place in Stanhope. His bride, Margaret (Peggy) Coltherd, (Coultherd), baptised on 13th February 1754, was the daughter of William Coltherd, who lived at

Windyside, St John's, Weardale. John and Peggy made their home in the Newbiggin area. They had a large family and when their son, John, was baptised on 20th May 1798 it was noted in the register that he was the 'fifth son of John Thompson, miner, native of Stanhope by his wife Peggy Coultherd, native of Stanhope.' This child was baptised two days after his birth, on 18th May 1798. There may have been an earlier child by the name of John, who died, and early in their marriage, in April 1788, and November 1789, they baptised two babies named Peggy, neither of whom survived. It was common practice for parents to 'pass down' a name from a deceased child, as family names were very traditional and important to them. Their other children were Matthew (October 1790), Hannah (October 1792), William (July 1795) and Joseph (February 1797). Peggy, John's wife died aged 55 in August 1810.

The Bell farmhouse in 2006

Life in Teesdale

Farming in Teesdale had never been easy. The elevation of the land was too high for arable, but the area was rich in lead ore, which had been mined in England since Roman times, mainly for its silver content. In Harwood-in-Teesdale in 1421 Roger Bainbridge was keeper of the lead mines, but in 1571 the land was forfeited to the Crown, because the then owner, the 6th Earl of Westmorland had taken part in the Rising of The North in 1569, when the Catholic Earl rebelled against Queen Elizabeth I and supported Mary, Queen of Scots. The Earl also lost his lands at Brancepeth and Raby Castle where, according to William Wordsworth;

'Seven hundred knights, retainers all of Neville,
at their master's call had sate together at Raby's hall'

The westernmost hills of the County of Durham are made up of limestone laid down in shallow seas over three hundred million years ago. Earth movements opened up cracks and fissures in the limestone into which flooded hot molten lava from deep below the earth's surface. As the lavas cooled they formed hard bands or 'sills' of basalt, the most famous of which is the Great Whin Sill. The heat of the lava baked the limestone into hard marble in places and, in Upper Teesdale, produced the 'sugar limestones' on which grow alpine plants such as the Blue Gentian. As time passed, natural chemicals in water passed through the rock and combined with the limestone to form new minerals such as lead and fluorspar. Further to the west, thick bands of sandstone lie on top of the limestone and, above them, peat and heather, which combine to give us the Pennine moors that stretch for miles.

Scientific methods for locating lead ore, or galena, weren't really necessary in the old days as there were one or two clues in the landscape to help locate the veins. Although geological knowledge must have been fairly rudimentary in the 16th century, most of the major deposits were known by then. Galena could be found in streambeds, particularly after storms and even lead-tolerant plants were looked out for. These clues often led to opencast mining, or hushing, which was one of the early methods used to obtain lead from the ground.

Robert Bowes and Charles Chaytor undertook a survey of the mines on behalf of Queen Elizabeth I in 1571. Like other mines, the Flakebrigg Mine at Eggleshope was in ruins and the indications were that the mine was worked out and had been abandoned, leaving the local population without work. The forsaken mine, and the crumbling ruins of workshops showed how entirely the industrial progress of the area had been checked. Any advancements that had been made in clearing the land for agriculture had also been lost and the people were destitute and living in poverty. German miners, brought over to England by Queen Elizabeth I, had just started work in the Vale of Newlands, near Keswick in the Lake District and they were introducing new and advanced mining techniques. In the 17th century the Bowes family had extensive rights to mine for lead in Teesdale and smelt ore. It is most likely that Robert Bowes hoped to benefit from this new knowledge and bring Teesdale mines back into production. He was, unfortunately, killed in an accident in the Keswick mines in 1610.

As it transpired, there was plenty of ore left in the ground, but there was no fuel with which to smelt the lead. The earliest recorded smelt mill is shown on a map of Eggleston dated 1614. The mill, located at Egglesburn, near to the present Blackton Bridge, is named on the map as 'Lady Bowes Lead Mylls' and was presumably operated by the Bowes family. It would have utilised all the techniques that were then known of the process of smelting, and peat and wood would have been used as fuel. The availability of the latter, however, was to become a problem. The earliest methods of smelting involved boiling, or smelting. The former, using a bole, involved burning ore mixed with brushwood and faggots within an encircling wall open to the prevailing wind. Smelting involved a more complicated process with a hotter fire, using a stronger draught produced by bellows with charcoal as fuel. The former, crude method was suitable for high quality ore, as was to be found in Weardale, and the latter process for the second quality and for reworking slag. The bellows were pumped by waterpower, but a great deal of fuel was needed for the actual smelting. Men had to cut wood, make it into charcoal and transport it carefully to the smelting mill.

A group of Quakers travelling on horseback in the dale came upon this situation and, with the characteristic benevolence of the religion to which they belonged, could not leave this scene of so much misery without considering some means of alleviating it. They decided to revive the lead mining industry in Teesdale, and consequently, the London Lead Mining Company, known by various other names including The London Lead Company and The Quaker Company, was formed in 1692 under a Royal Charter of William and Mary. In 1771 the company leased from the Hutchinson family at Eggleston Hall the two small smelt mills on Blackton Beck, which soon proved to be inadequate as the output from the reopened mines increased. They purchased a new site and established the Blackton Smelt Mill, designed by Robert Stagg, which was used for eighty years. The company took on extensive leases in Teesdale and, by the middle of the 18th century, had also acquired leases in Weardale, as well as in the Derwent Valley on the Durham/Northumberland border. Its main activity, however, was centred in Teesdale and the London Lead Company ultimately transformed Middleton-in-Teesdale into a thriving, small, industrial, company town, but they had a hard uphill struggle ahead of them, having to deal not only with the prejudices of an ignorant population, but also with the rudimentary style of ore production that they had inherited.

The Arms of the London Lead Mining Company

There was water in abundance, but machinery for washing the ore had not been invented and, for at least a century after the mines were taken over, all the washing was done by hand. The art of smelting had been so completely forgotten locally that the men of Teesdale had to be specially trained. In the meantime, the ores produced by the company were carried to the Whitfield and Acton Smelt Mills in Northumberland, a distance of nearly thirty miles, on the backs of Jagger Galloways, or 'gallowas', a now extinct breed of horse, which, for generations, provided the only means of transporting ore in an area where roads were few and far between. The company, however, was well financed and could afford to carry out experiments and, ultimately, in opposition to the opinion of the time that wood was indispensable to the process of smelting lead ore, they announced that it could be done through the use of coal. They consequently developed a coal-fired furnace for smelting lead ores with pit coal and sea coal. They introduced horse-levels in the mines, where horses or ponies drew the tubs. They located new veins, drained the existing mines to a greater depth and made underground haulage to a central ore-dressing and smelting site profitable. Their investment paid off and during the 18th and 19th centuries England became the world's main producer of lead and new uses were being found for it, thus increasing its value. It ultimately came to be used in paint enamel, glass making, shipbuilding and the manufacture of weapons in times of war.

The first lease in Teesdale was taken out on a number of mines in 1753 in the ore-rich Newbiggin area, near to where the Thompsons were already living and farming. By 1796 we are told that there were no fewer than fifty mines in the dale. The village of Newbiggin, the original meaning of which was 'new building', was an ancient settlement first mentioned before AD1200. In 1801 it was still a small community of 281 inhabitants, but sixty years later the population had increased to 641, as more people came to the area to find work. By then there were more 'new buildings' in the village, erected to house the increasing population, who had 107 houses between them. A school was built in the village in 1799 and, as there were Thompsons living both in the village and in the neighbouring area, it is likely that their children were educated there.

Some parts of the open moor were transformed as tracks were built to give access to the mine sites, where the mineshafts had to be excavated and dug out by hand before any ore could be extracted. Lodging shops had to be built, as did the various mine head buildings. In modern terms, the infrastructure had to be put into place before any ore could be removed. Side by side with these mining projects, quarries were opened to provide stone for all the building development that was necessary at the mine heads as well as for the construction of the smallholdings and houses for the workers. It was common practice for the stone to be quarried, where possible, in the immediate vicinity of the mine to avoid transport costs. The London Lead Company introduced stone arching into its mines in 1818 and, in 1827 it was ordered that 'all drawing levels, shafts and sumps are now constructed of stone'. The portals were framed in well-built masonry, commonly arched and sometimes with an inscription, or dated keystone. Most Teesdale buildings were constructed of gritstone, a brown-coloured Namurian sandstone, that was much easier to dress than the very hard whinstone. The two industries of mining and building on this scale in this remote area were new, and the available labour force was mainly unskilled, but the company had mines in other parts of the country so they could bring in their own stonemasons and carpenters if necessary. Modernisation continued with the introduction of iron rails into the mines in 1817 to replace the old wooden ones. They were laid in the levels, which were generally built six feet high (1.83m) and three feet wide (0.92m).

The old mines could still be used and the potential was there in the local geology to motivate the owners in this new development. Careful surveys were necessary for the location of ore-bearing veins. The instrument they used was probably the 'dial', which was a simple magnetic needle. It wasn't until about eighteen years after they leased the land for the Newbiggin mines that the London Lead Company opened their larger smelting mill at Eggleston, further down the valley. That made it possible for the new owners, for the first time, to finish off the process of lead ore production, efficiently, within the confines of the Upper Teesdale valley. They also processed ore from parts of Weardale, where they held leases on mines. This smelt mill at Blackton Mill, Eggleston, had its own local supply of coal not far away at Whitehouse, on Langleydale Common. Despite the development in the mines in the area since their resurrection, the Jagger Galloways, those strong horses with their heavy loads, were still the only means available to carry the ore to the smelter. They worked side by side with the men and gave their all in the struggle to extract lead from the Pennine hills. Each horse could carry two 'pigs' of processed lead, one on either side of a wooden pack-saddle, which was fitted with heavy leather saddlebags. Although carts pulled by one horse were used as early as 1805 to transport lead, the packhorse system continued in use until the 1880s. The processed lead was taken from Eggleston to Darlington where the old name Leadgate indicates the place where it was stored before being sold.

Work in the mines was extremely hard both for man and beast and, even though the people of the dale were grateful to have work, many of them had their lives shortened by their harsh working conditions. The mines opened up the valley and people flowed in from other villages and towns to find work in the now prosperous area around Middleton-in-Teesdale. At

Blackton Smelt Mill c 1900 (Photo: W F Heyes Collection)

the beginning of the 19th century the population of the town was about 800 people, but within thirty years it had risen to over 1,800. With the opening of the smelting mill in the small village of Eggleston, the population there went up from just over 300 to 788.

The London Lead Company was well known for its philanthropic activities in the north: it bought and regulated the price of grain when it was becoming expensive, encouraged and contributed to the sick clubs, which developed in most mining communities and provided houses and schools for the miners and their families. The company bought an estate in Middleton-in-Teesdale and began to transform the town. They built Middleton House, beside the road up to The Bell, in 1823. This imposing building housed the company's agent for Teesdale and Weardale as well as its office. Another fine house, by the same architect, was built in Stanhope, Weardale, in 1819 for the Weardale District Agent. A school was built near Middleton House in 1818-19, where the Bible was used both for religious instruction and to teach the pupils how to read. Land was purchased for the building of houses, both in the town, in the villages and the hamlets. These houses of various sizes were stone-built and of good quality but, as many of the tenants had large families, they often lived in very cramped conditions, with many children sharing one bed. There was an opportunity at this time for individual miners to purchase land from the company and build their own smallholdings. As the population was still rising and accommodation was in short supply, most of them built one or two small cottages onto their properties that they could let out to other mining families, which is what the Thompsons had done at The Bell, although, as it turned out, in their case they were able to accommodate many of their own family from time to time.

In most areas the miners were drawn from the partly farming local population and, because of the improvements then being made in agricultural methods, many scattered smallholdings and farms were built as part of the welfare system introduced by the company for its workers. They also held the idea that working on a few acres in their spare time would provide an antidote to the harsh working conditions endured by the miners.

Masterman Arch,
Masterman Place, c1890
(Photo: W F Heyes Collection)

Middleton House, c1910 (Photo: W F Heyes Collection)

These plots and houses were rented out and, in 1834 it was recorded that there were, on average, three acres of meadow and three to four acres of upland pasture. This was usually enough for two cows, or a cow and a Galloway pony, and it provided an additional source of income for the miners and their families. In this dual-economy system, the miners could become reasonably self-sufficient, producing fresh food for themselves and their families to help supplement what would, otherwise, have been a very poor diet. Miners' wives often took in lodgers, men of all ages, who needed accommodation.

Lead ore was mined between 1000ft (305 metres) and 2000ft (610 metres) and because of the remote location of some of the mines on the trackless Pennine moors, accommodation for the workers had to be provided at the mine sites in buildings called lodging shops, where they could stay during the week, sleeping on mattresses made of hessian stuffed with chaff or straw. They took with them enough food, carried in a 'wallet' or 'pillow bag', to keep them going until they could return to their homes, or lodgings, at the weekend. The diet of these men and boys was simple and consisted mainly of bread, bacon, eggs, 'crowdy' (oatmeal porridge), potatoes and hard peg cheese, made from skimmed milk. There was an abundance of fresh water from which they could make a hot drink. There may have been water in abundance, but stronger drink was not available to these men. The nearest beer shop or public house would be too far away for them and, besides, they wouldn't dare partake of strong drink during the working week for fear of losing their jobs. In 1842 it cost sixpence a week to lodge at the mine: four nights for the miners and five nights for the washers. The underground miners left on a Friday and the lead ore washers left on a Saturday. They usually slept at least two to a bed, were given leave to make 'crowdy' on the fire in the morning and have their potatoes boiled for them in the evening. A Dr Mitchell, from the Royal Commission of Children in Mines, wrote, in 1842, a contemporary account of life in a lodging shop. It described a mine about nine miles south from Stanhope, over the moors, so it was most likely in Teesdale. The conditions he found there shocked him. He knew that the beds had not been slept in for the three preceding nights

A typical 'lodging shop' - Ladyrake Mine, c1930 (Photo: W F Heyes Collection)

but the smell, to him, was utterly intolerable. There was little or no ventilation and he considered that the quality of the air in the dormitory-style room was worse than in the underground shafts of the mine itself. It is likely that, living not too far away from the mine and considering the cost of staying, the Thompson men and boys would make their way home at the end of their working day, weather permitting.

The price of lead was always liable to fluctuate and, in the 1830s, the price dropped sharply, because of cheap imports, and most of the small mines were unable to survive. However the London Lead Company had, by then, gained a foothold in the very rich mining area of Alston Moor and was one of the largest concerns in the Northern Pennines. When times were hard and men were laid off work, they were given employment building stone walls for enclosures and helping with the construction of turnpike roads. There were many working quarries in the area so there was an abundance of local stone for these projects. Waste from the mines was also used.

Men hand-picking bouse at Coldberry Mine
(Photo: Beamish Photographic Archive)

Boys standing at a 'picking belt' sorting ore (Photo: Beamish Photographic Archive)

The Quakers may have rescued the population from a life of poverty and they were diligent when it came to keeping their employees on the 'straight and narrow', but it was John Wesley and his followers who spread the Word of God amongst the people. Wesley himself preached in local houses in the dale in 1759 and Methodism soon spread throughout the region as more and more chapels were built. In 1759 a small piece of land was bought in Newbiggin from Robert Robinson by three of John Wesley's itinerant preachers and four local miners for the sum of £5. Here, in 1760, with the help of the local mining community, a chapel that has become the oldest Wesleyan chapel in continuous use was built, and over the years, even into his old age, Wesley continued to preach there occasionally. The Thompsons, however, in most cases, remained faithful to the Church of England but, unfortunately, the ancient 13th century Parish Church of St Mary, in Middleton-in-Teesdale, lost the fight against progress and was demolished in the 1870s to be replaced by the present Gothic edifice, built, probably, in the hope of rivalling the imposing large chapel buildings that were beginning to make their mark in the town. The new building, which cost just less than £6,000, had two windows from the old structure incorporated in its fabric, but the townspeople, on the whole, were distressed at the loss of their ancient church.

Newbiggin Methodist Chapel

Thompsons in the Dales

Fifth Generation

Thus it was that the next generation of the Thompsons, of Newbiggin, were living in the most important lead mining area in Teesdale at that time. Matthew Thompson (my great-great-great-grandfather) was the son of John and Peggy (Coultherd) and he was baptised in Middleton-in-Teesdale Parish Church on 23rd October 1790. He became a lead miner and married Margaret (Peggy) Horn on 3rd June 1813. Peggy, baptised on 17th March 1793, was the daughter of Jonathan and Hannah Horn of Middle Side, which was just down the steep road from Matthew's home, in the direction of Middleton-in-Teesdale. Some of Matthew's children were born at Middle Side, but eventually he and Peggy moved to The Bell, where they farmed eleven acres of land and brought up their family. Speaking in local dialect, Matthew would have referred to his home, as t'Bell, thus abbreviating 'the'. In the censuses over the years and in the registers of births, deaths and marriages, it is referred to, generally, as Bell. Some of the old farm buildings are still in use but many changes have taken place over the years. The farmhouse has been completely renovated and the adjoining cottages have had their windows and doors altered. A large house, which has a beautiful view across Teesdale to Holwick, has been built onto the end cottage.

Although Matthew's forebears had moved between Teesdale and Weardale, there were other branches of the Thompson family living in Teesdale, and at The Bell, during his lifetime. One John Thompson, who died in 1725, was referred to as a 'yeoman' and in his will he left 'all houses and land adjoining for life' to his wife, Ann. Another John Thompson, late of The Scar, Middleton-in-Teesdale, who died in 1812, also had a house to leave to his large family. It would seem that the Thompsons of Teesdale were reasonably prosperous. In the late 18th century improved breeds of sheep and better drainage extended the range of hill sheep farming. Both the local landowner at Raby Castle and the London Lead Company experimented with land improvement by draining and liming moorland. Previously the moors had been used for the grazing of stock, only, because many parts were too wet for sheep. The mining company itself was able to extend its building of farms and smallholdings onto previously unused, and unusable, land and to adopt the practice of erecting cottages with considerable enclosures of land and pasture to form smallholdings.

Like his neighbours, Matthew's farming year seldom varied and spring was a busy time. Lambing took place in April and then the ewes and lambs were put out onto the moors to leave the fields clear to be prepared for the hay crop. The cattle, which had been over wintered inside in the byre were 'loosened out' into the fields and pastures, in May. Animals no longer needed to be killed off and salted in the winter as they could now be fed on hay and root crops and their manure was spread on the fields when the ground was dry. Every few years the fields were limed. Cutting peat or 'peatin' was a seasonal event and every farm had its right to 'turbary, the digging of 'turf' or peat on the moors to use as fuel. This job was done in late May to early June and the cut peat was left to dry until September. Men did the cutting and the women and children did the stacking. Each family had its own place at the peat haggs on the moor where they did their cutting, and the peat could either be left stacked on the moor, or transported down to the farmyard. About forty cartloads would be taken and, in the days before coal was readily available, the peat, which was free, had to be made to last a whole year.

Sheep management took up a lot of the farmer's time. Clipping took place in the summer and the sheep also had to have their fleeces 'salved' or 'greased', a process by which each animal had a mixture of grease (sometimes butter) and Stockholm tar rubbed into it, both to waterproof the fleece and to kill 'kades' or grubs of the sheep fly, which were a menace. Each sheep was held on a salving stock, or wooden trestle, whilst its wool was carefully parted and its skin daubed with grease.

Haymaking was another family job and farmers also helped one another. Matthew was a miner, as were his older sons and he must have had some sort of agreement with the company to take time off to make hay, a job that could only be undertaken when the weather conditions were right. As many of the company's employees tenanted the small farms in Teesdale, on land which they themselves had improved by drainage, there could well have been a lot of men and their sons away from work for a short spell in the summer and this date couldn't be prearranged. The long scythe was favoured in Teesdale and it had a blade about five feet long and most of the men were proficient in its use. After the hay was cut it was raked into 'windrows' to dry and turned once or twice to let the air circulate. If the weather was fair and the grass dried quickly it was raked into pikes, which were then brought down to the barn on a pike-bogey, which was a horse-drawn implement on wheels. A hay-sledge was also used to gather hay in the fields. If the weather wasn't good enough to dry the hay it was left in cocks in the fields and re-spread until it was dry and could be stacked into pikes.

The farming year ended in November and December when the tups were allowed to run with the ewes, ready for lambing in the following spring. Winter weather was often severe in these parts and Upper Teesdale could be cut off from the rest of the world for long periods of time. Life came to a standstill as men with shovels proved to be no match for the deep, drifting snow, which blew in behind them as they cleared their farmyards and tracks and often buried their sheep. Their main priority at these times was to make sure that the other animals were fed and watered. 'The Great Storm' of 1825 was very prolonged and it brought real hardship to the area. It was said to have started in January and lasted for nineteen weeks, bringing heavy falls of snow over the Pennines. The winter of 1835 was almost as bad. In March the 'Liverpool & Newcastle' post coach and the 'Lord Exmouth' were snowed up on Stainmore and the 'London & Carlisle' coach was stuck in the snow near Brough. There was still snow on the hills on Midsummer Day.

The farmer's wife and daughters took care of the dairy, where the warm milk was put into large earthenware dishes and left until it 'creamed'. The cream was then skimmed off for making butter. It took the cream of three

George and Hilda Seaton (nee Thompson), Barry Seaton and his bride, Dorothy Saunders, and my maternal grandparents Jenny and Thomas Sydney Thompson

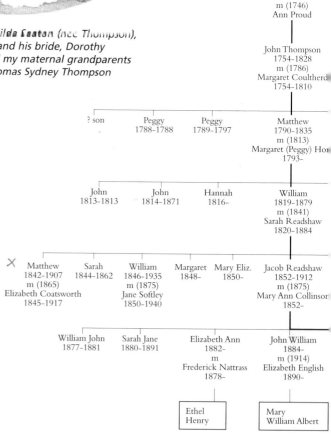

John Thompson
m (1663)
Elizabeth Bedell

John Thompson
1672-
m (1717)
Margaret Longstaff

John Thompson
1718-1783
m (1746)
Ann Proud

John Thompson
1754-1828
m (1786)
Margaret Coultherd
1754-1810

| ? son | Peggy 1788-1788 | Peggy 1789-1797 | Matthew 1790-1835 m (1813) Margaret (Peggy) Hor 1793- |

| John 1813-1813 | John 1814-1871 | Hannah 1816- | William 1819-1879 m (1841) Sarah Readshaw 1820-1884 |

| Matthew 1842-1907 m (1865) Elizabeth Coatsworth 1845-1917 | Sarah 1844-1862 | William 1846-1935 m (1875) Jane Softley 1850-1940 | Margaret 1848- | Mary Eliz. 1850- | Jacob Readshaw 1852-1912 m (1875) Mary Ann Collinson 1852- |

| William John 1877-1881 | Sarah Jane 1880-1891 | Elizabeth Ann 1882- m Frederick Nattrass 1878- | John William 1884- m (1914) Elizabeth English 1890- |

Ethel
Henry

Mary
William Albert

John Charters (husband of Mary), Mary Charters (nee Thompson, daughter of John and Lizzie Thompson), Albert Thompson (son of John and Lizzie) and Norma and Barry Seaton

Norma Seaton (later Smith), William Albert Thompson, Mary Thompson (later Charters), John Charters and Barry Seaton — in the woods at Bollihope Burn

Hannah	William	Joseph	John
1792-	1795-	1797-	1798-1867

Margaret	Ann	Jane	Jonathan	Mary
1822-	1826-	1828-	1831-1889	1834-
			m (1868)	
			Helen Neilson	
			1832-1893	

Hannah	Isabella	Jonathan	John	Sarah Ann
1854-	1856-	1858-1880	1860-1893	1862-

George Edwin	Thomas Sydney
1886-	1890-1956
	m (1911) ·
	Jenny Smith
	1892-1976

Ernest
Hilda (my mother)
May Harriet
Lily
Robert

My parents, Hilda and George Seaton, in the 1980s

gallons of milk to produce one pound of butter. The milk that remained after the separation was called 'blue milk' which was used to feed young calves, or, in the summer time, those families that kept a bacon pig would have a 'sour tub' which was a wooden or zinc barrel into which all the scraps from the table, the washing up water, potato peelings, apple peelings, vegetables, tea leftovers and churn milk went and when pigs were fed, this liquid was added. Most families had a pig which was bought in April at only a few weeks old and kept until October or November when it was killed, cured, and eaten over the following year. Any surplus butter or eggs could be sold in town on market day.

The original narrow lane out of Middleton-in-Teesdale that went up the Tees valley crossed the bridge over the Hudeshope Beck, near the edge of town, and climbed steeply up the hill to Middle Side. It then followed a wooded ridge that continued its upward gradient for a mile or more, passing The Bell and continuing high up above Newbiggin, past Ash Hill, down into Dirt Pit, up past Moor Riggs and eventually it reached Langdon Beck. In Matthew's early days at The Bell, the lane was the only way up the valley from Middleton-in-Teesdale, and it would have been very busy with everyday pedestrian traffic as well as the packhorses and their loads of lead ore. It was a laborious way of transporting the ever-increasing loads of raw material from the many mines up the Tees valley. Improvements to the road through Teesdale from Alston to the Abbey Bridge, near Barnard Castle in County Durham were much needed and they were authorised by Act of Parliament in 1824 as the result of a submission from the Greenwich Hospital, who owned the mining rights on Alston Moor. The improvements in Upper Teesdale, however, were delayed and funds were still being sought in 1831. The London Lead Company provided some of the necessary capital and the new road that was to take most of the mining traffic from the upper valley was finally built. There were still working mines high up in the neighbourhood of The Bell,

however, and they would have continued to use the old lane and packhorses to take the ore to the smelting mills at Eggleston. The hills behind Middleton-in-Teesdale and Newbiggin were criss-crossed by footpaths that were used by the miners on their daily trek from their homes and villages to their various places of work. A footpath ran through The Bell farmyard and further on a narrow lane lead down to the village of Newbiggin.

Matthew's and Peggy's last child, Mary, was baptised on 5th October 1834. Matthew was only 45 when he died in the following June. He made out his last will and testament on 4th June and signed it the day before he died. Jonathan Horn, Isaac Watson and William Thompson witnessed the will. He left his dwelling house with its adjacent buildings and the lands appropriated to the use of the household, his lands, tenements, hereditaments, which were any inheritable estate or interest in property and real estate, to his wife, Peggy, until her decease or second marriage. The same were to go to his three sons and their heirs as tenants in common. His daughters, Hannah, Margaret, Ann (Nanny), Jane and Mary were each left £10 to be paid to them by their brothers, after their mother's death when they reached twenty-one. Matthew also owned a farm at Turners, which was just off the road that led up the Hudeshope valley to the mines at

Turners farmhouse

43

Coldberry and Lodge Syke. Matthew stated in his will that this farm, including the lands, stints and hereditaments, had to be sold either by private contract or by public auction and the money raised was to be used to pay off all his debts, funeral and other expenses and the surplus to go to his wife, Peggy, towards the maintenance and education of his children. Peggy was still a young woman and she had been left with a large family. Isaac Watson, who was one of the witnesses to Matthew's will, was a neighbour, a lead miner, a bachelor, and a friend of the Thompsons, and he and Peggy were married on 10th December 1840, when he was 41 and she was 46. Probate of her late husband's will had been granted on 6th November, so the farm at The Bell, and the other properties passed to her sons. Peggy and Isaac went to live at Low House, Newbiggin, and they took Peggy's youngest child, Mary, with them. Matthew's brother, John, went to live at Turners, the other farm that Matthew owned. Matthew's early death was a tragic blow for the family but, in the five years following, more misfortunes were to strike the residents of The Bell. A Mary Thompson was the first to die. She was an 82-year old widow and the February of 1839 was her last. William Thompson, a relative of Matthew's, must have moved into the farmhouse after Matthew's death and he himself died there, at the age of 41 on 16th November 1840. His health had been deteriorating for some six months and he left behind a widow, Martha, and six children. Two other children of his also died at The Bell in the same year as their father: 11-month old Ann (Nancy) had died in February and her older sister, six-year-old Ruth, died from scarlet fever on 7th October 1840.

Sixth Generation

William Thompson (my great-great-grandfather), son of Matthew and Peggy, was born at The Bell and baptised on 4th July 1819, so he would have been only 15 when his father died. He married Sarah Readshaw in the parish church, Middleton-in-Teesdale, on 23rd December 1841. By that time he was a 22-year-old miner, living at The Bell with his 18-year-old sister, Elizabeth, their 12-year-old sister, Jane, and their 10-year-old brother, Jonathan Horn Thompson. These younger children had, for some reason been left behind at The Bell by their mother, Peggy when she remarried. Perhaps she didn't need to take them, as Margaret would have been capable, at 17 or 18, of running a household and it also meant that the family could stay on at The Bell, which William was to farm. Jane went on to become a housekeeper for a widower, James Balwin (Baldwin) from Scotland, who was a joiner, with a young family, living in New Town, Middleton-in-Teesdale.

In about 1852, young Jonathan Horn Thompson, William's younger brother, who was a leadminer, emigrated to Australia. He was an enthusiastic, adventurous, and optimistic 21-year-old and, with thousands of others from many countries around the world, he was off to take part in the Ballarat Gold Rush, which established Ballarat as a leading provincial city with fine buildings. Here, he met a young widow, Helen Neilson, who was born in Ayr, Scotland, in about 1832. Helen's first marriage was to an engineer, Walter Neilson, and they had a daughter named Helen, known in the family as Ellen, who was born in Glasgow in 1849. Mother and daughter had emigrated to Australia together. Jonathan would have moved about the goldfields surrounding Ballarat and Helen might have accompanied him despite the harsh conditions they must have encountered. They didn't marry until 1868, in Victoria, but they had several children together before then. Margaret Jane, their eldest, was born in 1856 and she withstood all the hardships of life in Australia at that time and died in 1943 at the age of 87. The rest of Jonathan's and Helen's children weren't as lucky. Walter, the next child, born to the couple in 1858, lived only five weeks. Frank Matthew and Walter James were twins and they both died before their first birthday. Sarah Jane, their next child, was born in 1866 in Maldon, near Ballarat, and she too died in infancy. Helen's daughter, Ellen, died when she was 12 years old in 1862, in the same year as the twins. Jonathan and Helen were buried in the same grave in Old Ballarat Cemetery; he on 5th September 1889, she on 13th March 1893. In the same grave their son Walter, aged five weeks, was buried and their grandson, Victor Mitchell, aged nine years. Margaret Jane, their only surviving child and mother of Victor Mitchell, had married Frederick Mitchell in Ballarat on 28th April 1880. They had seven sons and two daughters and spent the latter part of their lives in Melbourne.

Meanwhile, back in Teesdale, William and Sarah continued living at The Bell. In fact, they spent the rest of their married life together there, raising a large family and running the farm. The entrance to the cobbled farmyard was just beside the lane and William and Sarah occupied the double fronted farmhouse. Between 1842 and 1862 they had 11 children: five boys and six girls, all of whom were born at The Bell. Their names were Matthew (1842), Sarah (1844), William (1846), Margaret (1848), Mary Elizabeth (1850), Jacob Readshaw (1852), Hannah (1854), Isabella (1856), Jonathan (1858), John (1860) and Sarah Ann (1862). Jacob Readshaw Thompson was my great-grandfather.

Various tenants occupied the adjoining cottages during that time. In 1861 there were, somehow, three tenants; Hannah Scott, a miner's widow, lived there with her two sons, William and James, aged 19 and 17, who were both lead ore washers; a young servant girl, Elizabeth Horn, aged 16, completed their household; the two other occupants were Joseph Lee and John Allinson who shared their accommodation with their families. There were Thompsons living all around in the 1860s - at Dirtpitt, Stanhopegate, and Newbiggin. In that year the London Lead Company opened a new, and bigger, school in Middleton-in-Teesdale. The Thompson family were doing their best to increase the population. Thomas Thompson, a farmer and miner, and his wife Mary, living in Newbiggin, had nine children between 1851 and 1867 and their neighbour, Septimus Thompson, fathered nine children between 1841 and 1860, not all of whom survived. Combine these with the 11 Thompson children up at The Bell, born between 1842 and 1862 and you can quickly see why there were so many Thompsons in the area and why, between them, they have so many descendents. The mothers of these children would have had a big workload as their husbands had full-time jobs in the lead mines. As their children grew up, they too, would have had their regular jobs around the house and farm, although they would have had more permanent occupations before they were into their teens.

The 'new' 1861 School on Alston Road

On the other side of the lane from The Bell, a footpath led up and over the fields towards Hardberry Hill, passing Stoneygill High House and joining the track that led to the important mines at Coldberry and Lodge Syke, where William worked. The almost hidden valley of the Hudeshope Beck was very rich in lead ore deposits and had been plundered by the lead miners continuously for many years. Coldberry's recorded history went as far back as 1730 and there were signs of industry everywhere from hushes to large heaps of waste left behind after the lead ore had been extracted. William's and Sarah's oldest son, Matthew, started off his working life as a lead ore washer. After his marriage to Elizabeth Coatsworth in 1865 he lived in one of the cottages, near his parents, at The Bell. By the time he was 29 he was an 'overseer' in the mines and he and Elizabeth and their family moved to High Dyke, sometime between 1879 and 1881. He spent his whole working life in the lead mining industry, dying in 1907 at the age of 65, by which time he was living in Middleton-in-Teesdale. He had seven surviving children – four girls and three boys.

William's second son, named after his father, was still living with his parents and younger brothers and sisters at The Bell in 1871 when he was 25. He was a smelter of lead ore and perhaps, like many others, he would never have left the valley had it not been for the imminent demise of the lead mining industry. He moved from Teesdale to Sunderland to find work in the coal mining industry and married Jane Softley, daughter of Michael and Amelia Softley, of Bishop Wearmouth, Sunderland, in 1875. By 1881 he was a coal-teamer living at 5, Wall Street, Sunderland, with Jane and their one-year-old daughter, Sarah Jane. Later that year his wife presented him with another daughter, Henrietta, and a son, William, was born in 1885. With these three small children William and Jane emigrated to Australia in 1886 aboard the 'Almora' in search of a better life. They had three more children who survived infancy after they arrived in Melbourne, named Frederick, Jonathan Horn and Clarence. William's uncle, Jonathan Horn Thompson must have prospered in the Ballarat Gold Rush as he seems to have encouraged William to settle there. William's ship had terminated its voyage at Brisbane, Queensland, in 1887 and, after a short stay near there he and his family travelled south to Ballarat. One of William's sons, born in Ballarat in 1890, was baptised Jonathan Horn Thompson, after his great-uncle who had died in the previous year on 5th September 1889 at the age of 58.

The move to Australia may not have extended Jonathan's life by very much, but William certainly lived longer than he could have expected had he stayed behind in England. He died in 1935, aged 89, whilst his wife, Jane, was 86 when she departed this life in 1940. Each Christmas, William used to propose a toast 'To the absent ones', thinking of those of his Teesdale family who he never saw again, but at least he had had the guidance of his uncle when he first arrived in Australia. William's son, William, who was born in 1885, was in the Australian army during the First World War. He was stationed for a while in London and he did see his relatives again when he visited the family in Teesdale and Weardale. In later years they remembered him as 'Australian Bill'.

The Readshaw Connection

FOURPENCE A DAY

The ore is waiting in the tub, the snow upon the fell,
Canny folk are sleeping yet, but lead is reet to sell.
Come me little washer lad, come let's away,
We're bound down for slavery for fourpence a day.

It's early in the morning, we rise at five o'clock,
And the little slaves come to the door to knock, knock, knock.
Come me little washer lad, come let's away,
It's very hard to work for fourpence a day.

My father was a miner, he worked down in the town
'Twas hard work and poverty that always kept him down.
He aimed for me to go to school but brass he couldn't pay,
So I had to go to the washing rake for fourpence a day.

My mother rises out of bed with tears on her cheeks.
Puts my wallet on her shoulder, which has come to serve a week.
It often fills her great big heart when she unto me say,
I never thought thou would have worked for fourpence a day.

Fourpence a day, me lad, and very hard to work,
And never a pleasant look from a gruffy looking 'Turk'.
His conscience it may fall and his heart may give away
Then, he'll raise our wages to ninepence a day.

The next of William's and Sarah's sons was Jacob Readshaw Thompson (my great-grandfather) who was born on 2nd January 1852 at The Bell. He was named after his mother's father and brother, both of whom were Jacob Readshaws. There were Readshaws living and working in many of the lead mining communities in the area and they had been there for centuries. Sarah's branch of the family came from Hunstanworth, a small village in the Derwent Valley, in the north of the county, which can be reached by a narrow, moorland road from Stanhope. Sarah's father, Jacob senior, was the son of William and Mary Readshaw of Jaffrey's Rake, Hunstanworth, and her mother's parents were Robert and Elizabeth Bell of Blanchland, an historic village very close to Hunstanworth. Sarah could trace her family back to her seafaring great-great-grandfather, Captain John Readshaw, who lived in Aberdeen. He had married in Italy and my mother, Hilda Thompson, one of Sarah Readshaw's great-granddaughters, had obviously been told that she had Italian blood as she believed that both she and her father, Thomas Sydney Thompson, had inherited their black hair from a Mediterranean forebear. It seems she was right.

Jacob Readshaw and Sarah Bell were married on 17th September 1814 when they were both in their 30s. It was Jacob's second marriage. His first wife, Elizabeth Hamilton, whom he married on 5th June 1805 at Edmondbyers, a village only about four miles from Hunstanworth, died, leaving at least two small children - Bella, born on 14th October 1807 and William on 15th June 1810. Jacob's marriage to Sarah Bell produced Elizabeth in 1815, followed by John (1816), Mary (1818), Sarah (1820), and Jacob junior in 1824. All of these children were born in Hunstanworth, where Jacob worked in the lead mining industry. The London Lead Company owned the leases on lead mines in that part of the Derwent Valley and it was probably because they were expanding and improving their homes for miners at exactly this time in Middleton-in-Teesdale, that Jacob brought his family to Teesdale. He must also have had a good job offer as he took up the position of local Washing Agent for the London Lead Company. He and his family lived in Masterman Place, which was a rather imposing group of houses, built by the company to accommodate some of its more senior staff as well as cottages for the miners. In 1824 the company were advertising some of their smaller properties to let in Masterman Place for fourteen pence a week rent. Jacob senior had a long working life as he was still employed by the company in 1866 when he was 85. He outlived his wife, Sarah, by 28 years. His daughter, Mary, lived with him as his housekeeper, with the help of a servant girl until she herself died at the early age of 47, in January 1865. Jacob senior lived on for another five and a half years, dying in July 1870 at the ripe old age of 89.

One of his notebooks was found, quite recently, in a private collection, and is believed to be quite unique, as no other record of employees for the London Lead Company has been found to exist. Much of this notebook is to do with the supply of water to the various washing floors at the mines and the design of dams and such like, but it also contains handwritten information about applications for the positions of washer boys with the London Lead Company in Teesdale from 1862 to 1866. The washing of ore was an open-air task and, until 1834, it was traditionally the work of boys and women. After that date the boys had to do the job, working outdoors in all weathers. Children could cope with the workload, but after 1860, when the washing floors were mechanised, the physical effort required to complete a day's shift was lessened.

From the age of 12 to 18, as a rule, the boys had to attend the ore dressing (washing) floors. Their first task would be to pick out stones from the galena (lead ore). After the first year they were given heavier work such as wheeling 'bouse' and the 'deads' as the waste was called. By the fourth year of their employment they got to use the various mechanical separators. They could continue as washers until they had become familiar with the minerals they were separating, when they could become Master Washers, or, Mastermen Washers. During the three months of winter those aged 14 and over were allowed underground, whilst under 14-year-olds were sent back to school for the winter.

It was the policy of the London Lead Company, Jacob Readshaw's employers, to train local boys in all aspects of mining, although, perhaps because of his own elevated position in the company, two of his sons were spared an arduous working life. They both took up apprenticeships. John became a millwright and his job would have been to repair and maintain mill machinery, or even install it. After his marriage he moved to Nenthead in Westmorland, and then to Shildon, in County Durham, before returning to Middleton-in-Teesdale, where he and his wife, Dorothy, and their children settled down in California Row. He later became an engine fitter, as did his two sons, John James and Jacob, but before that the two boys did

35   *Applycations for*   *washing: 1866*

Boy's name	Abrode	Parent	yes no	Deceased parent	ages y m	marks
B Jos Hunt	M Place	Jno Hunt dead	yes		11 10	C B
Jos Tarn	Town End	Wm Tarn	yes		11 10	
A James Low	M Place	Egn Low	yes		12 9	C berry
B Henry Parken	M Place	Wm Parken	yes		11 4	
A Wm Denham	M Place	Geo Denham	yes		12 ~	C 22
A Geo Wilkinson	Beveley	Widow Wilkm	yes	Peter	12 2	
A Jno Cammone	Newbegin	Wm Cammone	yes		11 11	S 13
A Wm Parker	Townhead	Thos Parker	yes		12 11	S Raine
A Jos Lowes	Midleside	Thos Lowes	yes		12 -	C 13
Math Parkin	lane head	Widow Parkin	no	Will Parkn	14 8	
Isaac Wearmoth	Middlet	Hanah Wray	no	Illg	14 5	
Joshu Bussy	Town head	Victors Bussy	yes	Jno Bussy	11 11	
Wm Robinson	Hudshope	Wm Robmson	yes		11 7	
A Jno Tarn	Bowlees	Jno Tarn	yes		12 6	Redgrove
Jos Tarn	Do	Do	Do		13 11	Redgrove
A Wm Gargate	Gateside	Jno Gargate	yes		12 4	Kidgrove
A Jacob Tarn	Stangill	Thos Tarn	yes		13 -	Coldbery
Thos Allinson	Beveley	Jno Allinson	yes		12 2	

Extract from Jacob Readshaw's notebook (Photo: W F Heyes Collection)

Jacob Readshaw's painting of St Mary's Church, Middleton-in-Teesdale
(Photo: John Wearmouth)

a spell of ore washing.

The youngest son in the Readshaw family was Jacob junior, who was a man of many talents. He was a wood-carver, photographer, artist and amateur astrologer. The studio photographs he took, possibly with a camera he had made himself, were small, posed, Victorian portraits that could be used as visiting cards. He also took photographs of local buildings, in Middleton-in-Teesdale, such as the new railway station, opened in 1868. Three years later, in 1871, the Barnard Castle newspaper, the Teesdale

Jacob Readshaw (junior) (Photo: John Winter)

Mercury, reported that Jacob Readshaw junior had constructed a 6ft (1.83 metres) reflecting telescope for which he ground his own lenses. The dark skies of the Northern Pennines were unpolluted by street lights and, to this day, have England's largest area of darkness as seen from space. He was able to draw up a detailed map of the surface of the moon, which he later used as a basis for a papier-mache model of the lunar landscape, which was hung in a school in Middleton-in-Teesdale until earlier this century. Much of his furniture can still be seen in several houses in Teesdale, and in Middleton-in-Teesdale Parish Church he made the altar rails, the pulpit and a chair. A picture of the old Middleton-in-Teesdale Parish Church that he painted, still hangs in the church vestry. He also designed the original pulpit in the Methodist church.

Jacob Readshaw's oldest son, William, however, had not escaped the lead mines and he was a Washing Overman, living in Hilton, Westmorland, when his father died. He himself was 60 in 1871, so he had had to wait a long time for his inheritance. As the oldest son he inherited the bulk of his father's estate and he was able to leave his mining life behind him and return to Teesdale to farm. The land he inherited included

> 'Three fields, or closes, of freehold land and the houses thereupon, situated near Middleton-in-Teesdale and known by the name of Roseberry. The fields named the Longlands and the two rigs together with the parcel of land now enclosed therewith which was once part of Middleton Inner Pasture and gives right to win stones at the common stone quarries on that Manor'

All Jacob senior's printed books, wearing apparel and body linning (linen) were to be divided equally amongst his three sons, but all his written books and papers were to go to William. By 1881 William and Jacob junior were living next door to one another: William was a farmer at Roseberry, Snaisgill; and Jacob junior was a joiner and cabinet-maker, of Roseberry Cottage, employing four people, one of whom was William's 16-year-old son, James.

Competition for washer boy jobs, however, was a serious business as families were often large and employment had to be found for all these children. Apart from finding employment in the quarries, few alternatives were on offer for Teesdale lads. On the whole, if father was a miner, then so were his male offspring. The boys' parents or guardians put their names forward and the youngsters were usually assigned a lead mine nearest to their homes. Having a father working in the lead mines must have helped in the selection of these boys, to a certain extent and, in the case of Jacob Thompson, having a grandfather as Washing Agent almost guaranteed him a job. Each applicant was given a rating from A-C and Jacob achieved an A when, in 1864, at the age of 12 years and two months he was taken on to work with his father, William, at Lodge Syke Mine, which was up on the moor, just east of Coldberry Mine. Joseph Readshaw, son of another Jacob Readshaw and his wife Isabella, who was 12 years and six months old, was also found a place and he went to the Lune Mine. His father was a Lead Ore Foreman. There were at least eleven mines scattered over the area to choose from and, in 1864, there were 64 applicants for the job of washer boy, which was about average.

The raw material brought out of the mine was called 'bouse', which was a mixture of galena (lead ore), gangue (a name for other minerals such as fluorspar, which occurs with the galena) and country rock. Some galena is to be found in the limestone on the side of the veins. As much of the unwanted material as possible was left underground. The aim of the lead ore dresser, or crusher, was to produce as high a concentrate of ore as possible. For a good separation of 'bouse' it was essential that all the material should be reduced to particles of almost identical size. The first stage of ore dressing started with the removal of stone and spar, by hand. If the 'bouse' was fairly lumpy, boys worked at a 'knockstone' using 'spalling' hammers to break off obvious pieces of stone. The nuggets and clean ore were retained and the remaining waste was tipped into spoil heaps. The lead-bearing ore then went to be crushed, either by hand or machine, before entering the various separation processes. Not all mines were big enough to justify the expense of machinery for crushing ore and, in that case, their hand pickings would be sent to a dressing floor elsewhere in the valley. Roller crushers were introduced from South Wales in 1820. Like most other machinery available at that time, these crushers were water-powered and waterwheels of various sizes sprang up wherever lead ore was being dressed. When the 'bouse' had been broken down to a small, uniform size, it was spread out on filter beds and then subjected to several processes of washing, all designed to get rid of spar and stones and leave a clean concentrate.

The basis of the washing process was the great difference in the specific gravity of the ores, compared with the spar and stones. Whilst pure galena has a specific gravity of 7.75, barites has only 4.5, fluorspar only 3.2, calcite 2.6, and limestone about 2.6. The stream of water was allowed to wash away the rubble and leave behind the heavy lead ore, which sank to the bottom. In nearly every stage of the washing process, however, because of the brittleness of galena, some of the finer particles of the precious ore were carried off in the wash water, so settling tanks, otherwise known as 'trunks' were used. In these, constant stirring brought about a slight separation of the remaining particles of ore. This process was a job undertaken by boys or, on some dressing floors, a small waterwheel drove mechanical stirrers. With all the washing processes complete, the remaining ore was then loaded either onto the backs of ponies, or loaded into carts to be taken to the smelters.

Life expectancy in the mining communities was about 49 years in those days, and William and Sarah Thompson suffered the early deaths of three of their children. Their second eldest child, Sarah, who worked as a domestic servant, died on 4th May 1862, when she was 17 years old, from a disease of the bowels. Her mother was already expecting her last child when Sarah died, and the new baby girl, born on 29th November 1862 was, rather touchingly, baptised Sarah Ann. Jonathan, the third youngest in the family, who was a lead ore washer, died at the age of 22 from tuberculosis, whilst John, his younger brother, who had spent his short, working life as a quarryman, died from chronic bronchitis when he was 32. One of Sarah's relatives, 17-year-old George Readshaw, was killed accidentally at Coldberry Mine, where he worked, on Wednesday 18th February 1880. He suffered severe head injuries in a fall of rock within the mine itself, and another miner narrowly escaped injury. The Teesdale poet, Richard Watson, wrote a poem about this sad accident, which was produced as a black-edged memorial card. With this sort of mortality affecting other families in the dale as well, it is easy to see why life expectancy was so short. The miners who worked underground had their health undermined by a lethal combination of bad air, dust, fumes and general over-exertion in poor working conditions. The dust, damp, and bad air affected their lungs and caused asthma and bronchitis. Those who worked above ground and worked as lead ore washers had, at least, fresh air to breath, but their work was arduous and exposed to all the severity of the weather. With the quantity of water used on the job it was impossible to keep dry in the clothing that was then available. In the winter, conditions were made even worse when the water froze and many man-hours had to be spent breaking ice. Working in the quarries was just as damaging to the health of the workers who inhaled a lot of dust.

The Decline in Lead Mining

Despite their hard working life, come Saturday night, freshly scrubbed young men went out courting. Jacob Thompson was no exception and he didn't have far to go to meet his ladylove, whom he would have known since childhood, as she lived at nearby Stoney Gill. She was Mary Ann Collinson, daughter of Jane Collinson, who was a widow. Mary Ann was a small and slightly-built young lady and, in later life, she had to wear spectacles with blue tinted lenses as she had weak eyes. There had been Collinsons in the Middleton-in-Teesdale area since the 17th century and Mary Ann's mother, Jane, was a Collinson before she married. She had a hard life as her lead mining husband, William, died quite young and her eldest child, George, was described as an 'imbecile', in other words, he was mentally handicapped and was liable to have fits. As well as George and Mary Ann, Jane also had two younger sons, John and Thomas, and a second daughter, Elizabeth. She took in dressmaking as a means of supporting her family and she was helped in this by Mary Ann. Girls started school at age six and were expected to stay until they were 14, after which, some of them went into domestic service and many more spent the years until they married at home, helping their overworked mothers with the domestic chores and learning the basic, but very necessary skills of sewing, cooking, bread-making, washing, ironing and cleaning. For the eldest girls in a family it could mean a hard upbringing involving helping to bring up the youngest children. On the smallholdings and farms, these girls also had to milk cows, carry heavy pails of milk, feed animals, pluck chickens, skin rabbits, wash eggs, make butter and cheese and help with the haymaking. Many of them had their school days cut short because of problems at home, such as poverty, family illness or the loss of one or more parent. Girls were often taken in by other families and, although it seems rather grand to read of mining families with a servant girl, or two, they were often there because they had been given a home, as well as a job.

Seventh Generation

Jacob Readshaw Thompson, son of William and Sarah, married Mary Ann Collinson at Middleton-in-Teesdale Parish Church in 1875. They went to live at Stoney Gill and it was there that their first child, William John, was born on 10th May 1876. Jacob, who was a foreman of lead ore washing, still worked at the Lodge Syke Mine that was once one of the largest lead mines in the dale, employing about 100 men and 20 washer boys. 40 men could be accommodated in one of the lodging shops and 60 in the other. Another, smaller lodging shop had room for 20 washer boys.

In 1877/1878, however, the price of lead fell again, from £24 per ton to £18. In the first half of the 19th century Britain had been the world's leading producer of lead, and Teesdale and Weardale, as part of the North Pennine Orefield, were the chief centres of lead mining in the country, but industry in general was in serious trouble and the weekly pay for the miners reflected the drop in lead prices, dropping by one shilling a week to fifteen shillings. Unfortunately, this downturn in production coincided with Lodge Syke Mine becoming worked out and, by the mid 1870s it was closed down. Over 100 men and boys lost their jobs in the Lodge Syke closure and many others were to follow, as one mine after another faced extinction. High Skears Mine, also in the Hudeshope valley, had been highly productive in its time, but it had to close in 1879. These mine closures brought extreme poverty throughout Teesdale. The workhouse was full and relief funds were set up to feed the hungry. Dairies could not sell their milk so they reduced the price from twopence to a penny, claiming as they did so that they and the milk-producing farmers would go bankrupt. The London Lead Company was big enough to support a certain amount of loss, but the end was in sight for the industry. The people of the dale had little alternative but to find work elsewhere, many of them taking the big step of leaving England altogether, as many others before them had had to do, heading for Canada or Australia in their search for a better life.

William Thompson, Jacob's father, died on 7th April 1879. He had given up mining by that time and was farming his 11 acres of land, but he would

Skears hushes (Photo: W F Heyes Collection)

Low Skears mine, c1890
(Photo: W F Heyes Collection)

have been devastated and depressed to see the decline of the Teesdale lead mining industry that had been his life, and the life of most of his forebears and family for longer than he could remember. There were still mining jobs to be had, however, in this once important industry, and at least two of his daughters married miners. Hannah's husband, Robert Grieve, whom she married in about 1880, was one of them. He was still mining in 1891, as were many of his neighbours at Aukside, but by the time he was in his 40s, in 1901, he had become a whinstone quarryman. Sarah Ann, William's youngest child, who was a dressmaker, and still living at home when her parents died, married Joseph Collinson, also a lead miner, in 1888. Mary Elizabeth, the second oldest of the sisters, broke with tradition and married John Gibson, a gamekeeper, and they went to live near Staindrop. Margaret married John Allinson, a joiner from Middleton-in-Teesdale, in 1869. It's not certain what became of Isabella, who was aged 15 and still living at home in 1871. Did she marry, or remain single, or suffer the fate of her two younger brothers, Jonathan and John, who both died young? Jonathan died the year after his father, in 1880, and John died in 1893.

In his will, William had left *'All his freehold houses, lands and tenements, hereditaments, and premises situated at The Bell'* to his sons. The profits and the rents were to go to his dear wife, Sarah, *'for her own absolute use and benefit of her natural life as long as she continued as his widow.'* Legacies of £30 were left to each of his daughters, Margaret Allinson, Mary Elizabeth Gibson, Hannah, Isabella and Sarah Ann Thompson. If Sarah, his wife, wished to carry on farming as they had been doing, his sons had to allow her to do so, instead of paying to her the rents, issues and profits. His furniture, goods and chattels were to be divided up amongst his daughters. It is interesting that William lists his books and pictures separately, so they must have been of some importance to him. They, and his *'monies, securities, farm stock, farming and dairy utensils, together with the residue'* were to go to Sarah, his wife, *'for her use and benefit during the term of her natural life, or widowhood and, at her decease, or second marriage, to be divided amongst his sons.'*

Sarah, who had already had a small legacy of £100 from her late father, Jacob Readshaw, chose to stay on at The Bell and she continued farming with the help of her family. She died at home at the age of 63 on 27th October 1884, with her eldest son, Matthew, at her bedside.

The iron waterwheel with wooden spokes at Coldberry Mine
(Photo: Beamish Photographic Archive)

Coldberry Mine (Photo: Beamish Photographic Archive)

Weardale

By 1880, from necessity, Jacob and Mary Ann had left Teesdale. Their journey, however, was shorter than that taken by many other Teesdale families at that time. It took them on the rough road over the moors that linked Middleton-in-Teesdale with Stanhope, a distance of about twelve miles. As the family were only going as far as Bollihope, they could have left this road after about eight miles and used one of the many tracks over the peaty moors that linked the lead mining communities of both valleys. Alternatively, they could have taken the Frosterley road that was a little further on. Most of these tracks over the moors have fallen into disuse, but in those days, when they were in regular use they were properly maintained by gangs of road menders, who were employed to repair the surface and fill in the potholes. One track led down to Whitfield Brow and Bollihope, where the London Lead Company held the lease on a lead mine. From that turn-off point, the young Thompson couple would have been able to see their new home in the distance as the track went down the valley close to the Howden Burn, past a quarry and the lead mine workings and on to Whitfield Brow and Bollihope, where Jacob had secured a good job as Lead Ore Washing Master, or Washing Master, at the Cornish Hush Mine.

The road from Middleton-in-Teesdale joined the Eggleston to Stanhope road that had once had an importance of a different kind as it was built, originally, by the Romans, and the area was, at one time, inhabited by the Romano-British, whose remains, and the remains of their huts, have been found and excavated on Bollihope Moor, near Bollihope Burn, close to where a road branches off to Whitfield Brow. Some lead slag from the site was sent to the University of Oxford to be radiocarbon dated, and the results have shown that smelting had taken place on the site some time between AD880 and AD1030. This predates the earliest historical records of lead extraction in the county, and Bollihope Common is now the earliest known lead-working site in the region.

The Eggleston road, which was built in the early 1800s by the London Lead Company, overlies the Roman road, which continues its course

Old mine building at Whitfield Brow

northwards, over the ford on the River Wear at Stanhope, and on to Corbridge and the Roman Wall. The moors had more natural ground cover and tree growth in Roman times and would have been frequently used then, not just as a highway, but as a hunting ground. A Roman altar, erected by a cavalryman, Micianus, was found in the area. It is dedicated to Silvanus, the woodland god, in thanks for having 'taken an elusive giant wild boar'. The successful hunting party were from the Sebosian Cavalry, who were stationed first at Binchester and then in Lanchester, both on Dere Street, in County Durham. The importance of the Wear Valley as a hunting ground continued through the centuries, when the Bishops of Durham took their sport, hunting for wild boar, hare and deer.

William the Conqueror had made the 'Bishopricke of Durham' into a County Palatine, giving the Norman bishops, who he had installed there, the rights of Prince Bishops. The king needed a strong, loyal force between England and Scotland, and the earliest cathedral at Durham had a powerful religious significance as a place of pilgrimage. The king himself had paid homage there at the tomb of Saint Cuthbert. From their palace at Bishop Auckland, and their castle and cathedral on the River Wear at Durham, the bishops had easy access to their deer parks in Weardale. Altogether, in the 12th century, 60 square miles in Weardale was set aside for hunting, and great chases were held regularly by the bishops. However, times were changing, and by the 13th century, when more land was needed for farms, the deer were confined to an enclosed park, the east and west gates of which are now marked by the communities of Eastgate and Westgate.

'Hope' as in Bollihope, Ireshopeburn, Rookhope and Hudeshope, is of Anglo-Saxon origin and means 'side valley'. Bollihope (Bollyop) itself is now no more than a small farming community, but it once had a church, or chapel, as did Bishopley (Bishops) that was just a mile or two down the road towards Frosterley, a name probably derived from 'Forest lea', an ancient village mentioned in the Boldon Book, which was the Bishopric's equivalent of the Domesday Book. Stone had been quarried and dressed in the area as far back as 1183 and quarries still abounded, one of which, the Harehope Quarry, on the eastern outskirts of Frosterley, was once the main source of the famous Frosterley marble that adorns many cathedrals, including the Chapel of Nine Altars, at the eastern end of Durham Cathedral, where it has been cut and polished into a series of slender pillars in the 'Early English' style of arcading. It is not a true marble, but limestone, full of coral fossils, which can be polished. By the 12th century, King Stephen had granted mineral rights to Weardale, and the church had particular need for lead, as it was used extensively on the roofs of churches and cathedrals and for water cisterns, pipes and gutters. The Prince Bishop's Office either organised their own mining, or leased out the mines. As the lead in the area was of high quality and rich in silver, averaging 9oz (255g) to a ton of lead, it was worth exploiting, as the bishops had their own mint in Durham.

In Weardale, the major exploiter of lead production was the Blackett-Beaumont Company, begun by Sir William Blackett in Allendale in 1684, and later passing to the Beaumont family. Its earliest mines were leased from the Bishop of Durham and, in the early 1700s Sir William Blackett was the bishop's Moormaster in Upper Weardale. The company later owned mines of its own and had its headquarters at Newhouse, near Ireshopeburn. With business and capital connections the London Lead Company and the Blackett-Beaumont Company were able to introduce more advanced techniques, for example relating to drainage.

There were six purpose-built houses at Whitfield Brow, Hill End, Frosterley, Weardale, all with long gardens, where the tenants could grow their own fruit and vegetables. The house on the end, furthest away from Frosterley, was a farmhouse, where George Wallace lived. He farmed seventeen acres, but he was also a Lead Mine Agent. The other families living there in the early 1880s were those of John Walton (lead miner), William Robinson (engine keeper driver), Jeremiah Anderson (brakes man on the railway), and William Watson (lead miner). Jacob Thompson had a new title, but he was doing the same job. He was now called a Lead Ore Washer Manager.

There are few signs, now, to show that the land surrounding Whitfield Brow was a small, thriving industrial site when Jacob and his family arrived and he virtually lived on the job. He worked at the Cornish Hush Mine, which, together with the Whitfield Brow dressing floors, formed part of the London Lead Company's Bollihope development. A hush mine took its name from the old, simple opencast method used for both prospecting and working. This method was almost unique to the steep-sided valleys of the Pennines and parts of Wales. Water was collected behind a dam, above an outcrop vein, and then released, scouring the lead ore to a lower level. A hush could be as long as half a mile and up to one hundred feet deep. Lead ore (galena) and fluorspar are usually found together in 'pipes' or 'rakes' which fill vertical fissures between the harder rocks and they can, sometimes, reach to great depths. A vein cut by a hush would be repeatedly loosened with picks, and then washed out by another hush, the ore being sorted at the foot of the slope. This process is the cause of the large size of some of the ravines which can still be seen on the Pennines. Some of these hush mines were still being worked in the 1890s, but many of the mine leases forbade this type of exploration by then as it was inefficient and wreaked destruction on the landscape. The Cornish part of the name 'Cornish Hush' came from the large number of miners who came north

Cornish Hush Mine dressing floor and mine building

1'10" locomotive 'Sampson' ran between Cornish Hush and the Whitfield Brow dressings floors (Photo: W F Heyes Collection)

from Cornwall to find work in the lead mines. At one time, many of them lived in one street in Frosterley. Their wives were well known for their talent of lace making, a skill that they passed on to the other women in the town.

Technology was quite well advanced by this time and a 1'10" (56cm) gauge locomotive, called Sampson, ran between the mine at Bollihope and the dressing floor, where the impurities from the rock were removed at the washing rake. The locomotive had a two-cylinder engine and was capable of hauling heavy loads of ore down the valley. Built for the company in 1874 by Stephen Lewin, it came from the Poole Foundry in Dorset. The main Wear Valley railway itself had been built as far up the valley as Frosterley as early as 1847 and the North Eastern Railway's Bishopley Branch ran to within about a mile of the dressing floor at Whitfield Brow. There may have been a rail link between Bishopley and Whitfield Brow and it is possible

that a later road was constructed on the track-bed. When the mine closed and the track was taken up, the locomotive was either sold or scrapped, and its fate is unknown.

The Walton family ran the Bollihope Smelting Mill. John and Joseph Walton, sons of Jacob Walton, were Lead Mine Agents who came originally from Alston. They established themselves in the Stanhope-Frosterley area, where they had lived since the early 1830s and, between 1840 and 1850 their family business owned the freehold on lead mines at Brandon Walls, East Dryburn and Bollihope. The Bollihope Smelt Mill, located no more than a mile or so away from Whitfield Brow, in the valley bottom, on the banks of Bollihope Burn, had been offered for sale by auction in March 1831. It isn't known who bought it, but soon afterwards it was being run in the name of Jacob Walton & Co. By the mid-1840s Joseph Walton, who lived at Bollihope House, near the smelting mill, was in charge, processing ore from the family-run mines in Weardale and Alston. He became lessee agent for Hollywell Lead Mine, half a mile from Frosterley, which produced 321 tons of galena between 1848 and 1857. John, his brother, was proprietor of the mine. Bollihope Smelt Mill was first leased by the London Lead Company in 1855 and so the galena from Whitfield Brow dressing floors could well have been processed there, rather than being transported back to Teesdale.

As we know, the British lead mining industry continued to decline after

1860 due to foreign imports, chiefly from Spain. The price of lead dropped considerably, causing a recession from which the mines never recovered. In some mining communities in the Northern Pennines the population dropped by as much as 40-50%. The Blackett-Beaumont Company relinquished its Weardale leases in 1880, but lead workings continued for a while as some of their leases were taken over, either by the Weardale Lead Company, which was formed in 1883, or by the miners themselves. By the 1890s the Bollihope Smelting Mill, which was still in family ownership, was finally closed down by Jacob Vickers Walton. The last phase of the lead industry, which extended the lives of some of the Weardale mines, benefited from the secondary extraction of fluorspar, previously discarded as waste. Fluorspar was important as a flux in the steel industry and also as a source of fluorine-based chemicals and it was mined extensively in Weardale during the 20th century, the last mine closing only recently. Yet again, cheap foreign imports made the industry non-viable.

By 1890, Jacob Thompson was 38 years of age and living in the house next to the farm. His family was complete, but later the following year his second child, Sarah Jane, who had been born at Whitfield Brow on 31st May 1880, shortly after the family arrived in Weardale, died at the age of 10 from tubercular meningitis, after being in a coma for three days. Jacob and Mary Ann had already suffered the loss of their eldest son, William John, who had died from gastric fever, at the age of five in August 1881, again, shortly after they arrived in Weardale. Their surviving children were Elizabeth Ann (born 1882), John William (1884), George Edwin (1886) and Thomas Sydney Thompson - my grandfather – who was born in 1890. The older Thompson children, together with the offspring of their neighbours, attended the local school, which was two miles away at Frosterley. To get there, the children, no doubt in the care of the older girls, had to walk the steep road up and over Hill End, which would have been busy with horse-drawn vehicles from the quarries and mines for most of the year, but sometimes impassable to both pedestrians and road traffic in the winter, when really deep, drifted snow could cut off the communities, mines, quarries and farms for days on end.

The London Lead Company surrendered its leases on the Cornish Hush Mine in 1883, though the mine continued working in a small way. In 1891 some of the families had moved on, but despite the crisis in the lead ore industry, this small community now had 24 children living at home, five of whom were lead miners, as were their fathers. Jacob Thompson was the only non-miner at that time as he had turned his hand to working as a carpenter at a quarry. George Wallace still lived in the farmhouse at Whitfield Brow and he was referred to as a Lead Mine Overseer. The mine office was in one of the front rooms of the farmhouse, overlooking the garden, where there were displayed some large ornamental pieces of rock, found in the mine, that glistened with spar in various shades of purple. George Wallace died in 1893 aged 65 and, presumably, Jacob Thompson applied for the tenancy of the seventeen acre farm and farmhouse as, in 1894, he was referred to as a farmer, although he was now working at the mine, again, and was employed, again, as a Lead Ore Washer Manager. By 1901 Jacob was the only head of family living at Whitfield Brow who was still employed in the lead ore business. He was said to have become a Director of the Bollihope Lead Mine.

His farm buildings were separated from the farmhouse by a small patch of grass on which a hen house stood. Rough, often windblown, heather-covered moors surrounded the houses and a rough track wound its way down the hillside, past the dressing floor and narrow gauge railway track, to the road and the river in the valley bottom. There weren't any fields near the farmhouse; these were to be found on either side of the road. His farm was mechanised, to a certain extent, but he still needed a heavy horse, or cart-horse, to pull the grass-cutter and other equipment, but that work, and the hand-turning of the grass at hay-time had to be done against the clock, as the weather in Weardale, as in Teesdale, was usually unreliable. It was literally a case of 'make hay while the sun shines', and sometimes the sun didn't shine long enough and the valuable crop would be spoilt by rain as it lay in the wet fields. Farmers still helped one another, as they had in the past, and there were always extra hands available at times such as haymaking, sheep gathering and clipping. Jacob kept a few cows for milk and he had a small flock of tough Swaledale sheep that roamed the hills until the various times of year when they were gathered for dipping, dosing, clipping and all the other chores necessary to keep the animals healthy and ready to reproduce a new crop of lambs.

In the back corner of the farmhouse, with a door opening directly into the backyard, there was a dairy where Mary Ann had her shiny, metal milk separator and churn. It was here that she made butter from the separated milk in a much more efficient way than her forebears had been able to do. The cows were brought up from the fields to the byre where they were milked, which was often her job. She then had to carry the heavy pails of fresh milk to the dairy. In their long front garden the family grew potatoes, vegetables and fruit, such as gooseberries and rhubarb. There was no electricity either in the farm buildings, or in the farmhouse, so oil lamps had to be filled every day and their wicks trimmed. These country people were very good at 'make do and mend' and nothing was thrown away, or replaced, until it was completely worn out. Soles of shoes, clothes and even metal pails were patched, and hand-made woollen socks and jumpers were darned repeatedly. Any redundant material was kept, cut into strips and made into hard-wearing mats and rugs for the house. Mary Ann took in dressmaking, and she no doubt regularly re-modelled old clothes, as well as making new garments, both for her family and her customers.

There were many less children living in the six houses by the turn of the century and the place must have been strangely quiet. Before then, Jacob's oldest surviving son, John William (known as John) was working in the mining industry back in Teesdale, in the traditional family job of lead ore washer. He was 17 years old in 1901 and he was boarding at the home of his mother's sister, Elizabeth, and her husband, Joshua Bussey, a grain warehouseman, and their family at 8 Hill Terrace, Middleton-in- Teesdale. Elizabeth and Joshua had two children, Mary Jane and John, who was an apprentice cabinet-maker and was the same age as John Thompson. Elizabeth's oldest child, Margaret Ann had died at the age of 11 in 1889. Elizabeth and Joshua had lived at Stoney Gill before moving to Middleton in 1891. They were living there when Elizabeth's mother, Jane, went to live with them.

Back at Whitfield Brow, only two of Jacob's family were still at home. John's younger brother, George Edwin, aged 15, was apprenticed as a fitter in the steelworks, and Thomas Sydney, his youngest brother was an 11-year-old schoolboy. Jacob's only surviving daughter, Elizabeth Ann, was married to Frederick Nattrass, from a neighbouring family, by the time she was 19, and they eventually moved to Whitfield Brow, living in the house next to the farm. The Nattrass family had been around in Weardale and Teesdale for many generations. William Nattrass, with two other men, held a lease on a mine in Upper Weardale as early as 1425. Edmund Natras was Rector of Middleton-in-Teesdale Parish Church in 1536. Ralph Natrass had a pew in St Mary's Church, Middleton-in-Teesdale in the 16th century, as did Cuthbert Nattrass of Newbiggin. Frederick's family, however, were far removed from these privileges and were almost all employed in the limestone quarries. In later years, his only son, Henry, also a quarryman, died at the age of 21 from cancer of the knee, caused by being injured by a falling rock.

The London Lead Company was still in business and it carried on trading until 1905 when it went into liquidation, but by then many ex-miners had found jobs in the quarrying industry, which had been important to the Weardale economy since about 1830, when Lanehead Quarry, Stanhope, began to supply limestone to the Derwent Iron Company. Other main limestone quarries, such as Bishopley and Bollihope were operating by the 1850s. Ironstone quarries were also developed at Middlehope and Rookhope and, by the latter part of the century, quarrying activities in Weardale were extensive.

Jacob Thompson would have had little time for hobbies as, like most men of his day, much of his time would have been taken up by doing practical chores, making and mending as he went about his daily work on the farm. He did have time, however, for his role as leader of the Stanhope Silver Band, founded in 1823. As far back as 1835 the London Lead Company had encouraged and subsidised the formation of brass bands and helped with the cost of instruments and, by Jacob's time, they were thriving in all the Dales' towns. The Thompsons, like many other Victorian families, had an organ, or harmonium, in their parlour that the children were taught to play. Little did they think that these musical talents would be used in the ways in which they were, particularly by my grandfather, Thomas Sydney, who had served an apprenticeship as a joiner, before going on to be a bugler, in the army, in the First World War. When he returned home, in order to increase his income, he worked in the evenings in a cinema, in Shildon, where he lived, playing the piano as an accompanist to the silent films.

Jacob Thompson's life as a farmer was short lived, as he suffered from kidney trouble and he died at his home at Whitfield Brow in May 1912, at the age of 60. His oldest son, John, was back from lead mining in Teesdale and he took over from his father on the farm. He lived there with his mother until he married. He didn't rush into matrimony and he was a 32-year-old bachelor when he and Elizabeth (Lizzie) English were married in Wolsingham Parish Church on 13th June 1914. By this time John's two youngest brothers had left home: George Edwin eventually became a schoolmaster at Corporation Road School in Darlington; Thomas Sydney married Jenny Smith, my maternal grandmother, in 1911 and by the time he went off to war, he had two children, Ernest born in 1912 and Hilda, my

The houses at Whitfield Brow in 2006. The dressing floor was in front of them.

mother, who was born 10th June 1914. As it turned out, June was a month of civil unrest in England, when two million workers, including miners, builders and railway workers were on strike and, little did they know that before the end of the year, many of them would be in the army, as Britain declared war on Germany in August 1914, and a British Expeditionary Force of 70,000 men was immediately mobilised and sent to France.

John and Lizzie Thompson

Eighth Generation

John Thompson was my great-uncle. His new wife, Lizzie, came from Wolsingham, where her father, John English, was a carpenter. She was 24 years old when she married John and was living at home, where she was one of a large family. She was already used to hard work before she came to Whitfield Brow, and she would have been a good help to Mary Ann, her mother-in-law, who was, by then 62, and would have been grateful for an extra pair of hands to help with the daily round of chores. Wearing a long skirt and an old woollen cardigan, Lizzie was soon clomping about the yard in her clogs, as she took over the outdoor work. She raised only two children: Mary was her oldest child and William Albert, the youngest. Albert was born after the end of the First World War, in 1922. There was nothing of the fat, jolly farmer's wife about Lizzie. She was thin and she and John were very similar in appearance in that they both had typical, craggy Dales faces. Mary resembled her parents, but Albert, in his teenage days was fair-haired, with a round face. John was a man of few words, in fact the only words I remember him saying were addressed to his dog, Spot, when he told it, in Dales dialect to 'Gee ower scratten.' (Stop scratching!)

He had hardly ever been anywhere, apart from Middleton-in-Teesdale, to gain experience of anything except the life he had had as a lead miner and the life he was living, now, as a farmer. He had never seen the sea, or driven a car in his life and things continued unchanged on the farm, except for the death of his mother, Mary Ann, between the war years. He wore clogs to work, an old collarless shirt and a small, narrow, once-white, hand-knitted scarf at his throat. A waistcoat and a thick pair of trousers completed his daily wear, and when he was outdoors in cold weather, these were covered by a threadbare overcoat that had seen better days and which was fastened round the waist by a bit of twine. In wet weather an old hessian sack was often fastened round his shoulders to give a bit of extra protection against the rain and snow. A shepherd's crook and a cloth cap completed his outfit and, with his dog at his heels, he plodded along, with his head down, resembling just about every other man of his age in the valley, as he went about his farming business.

John and Lizzie weren't destined to have a prosperous life together, and they had to be frugal, as there wasn't much profit to be made in farming seventeen acres but, once war was declared, every effort had to be made to produce as much food as possible. Many young men went off to war, so there was less help available, but farming was important to the nation. It was a hard life and every outdoor job they did was reliant on the weather. One wartime winter was particularly bad. It was recorded that on 8th October 1916 it began to snow and there were fresh falls every day until April 1917. In mid-May, Wolsingham houses still had 9 inches (229mm) of snow on their roofs; snowfields in the Bollihope valley lingered until June. As expected, there were heavy losses of sheep for the farmers in that severe winter. Basic requirements such as flour, sugar, lamp oil and animal feed were usually bought in large quantities, but supplies must have run short in that particular year.

With the lead mine closed and the parent company in liquidation, most of the signs of mining were being removed from Whitfield Brow by this time. All the railway tracks and mine machinery were taken away for scrap, leaving behind the waste tips and the remains of the dressing floor. Change came, again, when World War Two started in 1939. Many children in England were being evacuated from the towns and cities to the safety of the countryside. Many others, including my future husband, Peter Smith, went either to Canada or America. Peter left Darlington for Toronto, Canada, when he was a 10-year-old boy and didn't see home, again, until he was 15. Barry, my brother, my paternal grandmother (Nana) and myself went to stay with John and Lizzie at Bollihope, but we were back home again, in Darlington, within a few months. Nana, who lived with us in Darlington, was considerably unnerved by air-raid shelters and potential air raids, and was happy to go with us, both for her own safety and to help with our every-day care. With our parents, Hilda and George, we boarded the train from Darlington's North Road Station to Frosterley, from where we took a pony and trap to get us, and our few possessions to Whitfield Brow. I seem to remember that my father, Barry and I walked most of the uphill bits, as the pony had a hard job pulling us all up and over Hill End, on our way to a few months' adventure and freedom.

There was a reservoir on the hill behind the houses, which must have been there for the use of the mine, which needed a lot of water to wash the ore, but there was no water supply to the houses, farmhouse or farm buildings at Whitfield Brow. The farmhouse water supply came from a spring, and in the washhouse, in the yard behind the house, there was a large, stopped-up cast-iron bath, full of icy-cold water, which was ladled out as required. There wasn't a sink in the kitchen either, only a chipped enamel bowl that was kept on a small table behind the backdoor, near the pantry. The usual kitchen range took up about a third of one wall and a peat, or coal fire was kept burning all the time. A small boiler in the range was filled up with cold water from the washhouse, and it was heated until required for washing up, or for filling the tin bath on bath-night. There was also an oven in the range for baking bread and cooking the family meals. A kettle hung on an iron hook over the fire, and a kitchen table stood in front of the window, on which Aunt Lizzie did her baking and ironing, using the fire in the range to heat up her 'dog' or piece of iron, which was heated until red hot in the fire and then placed in her box iron, before being secured by a lid. After ironing, the clothes were put on an airing rack, which was pulled up almost to ceiling height, in front of the fire.

A long settle and a grandfather clock stood against one wall, through which a door led into the parlour, a room full of Victorian furniture that was hardly ever used. It was kept for best, and, like the rest of the house, if a fire hadn't been laid in the grate, the room was usually cold. The kitchen, on the other hand, was always warm and the family seldom changed out of their working clothes unless it was a Sunday, or market day, or a special occasion. Through from the parlour were the stairs, at the foot of which were tied-back lace curtains. Home made rugs were scattered about the wooden bedroom floors and the big, heavy Victorian brass beds were complete with feather-filled mattresses, blankets, and fresh-smelling white sheets and pillowcases, that had been dried out in the open area beside the house, in the usually brisk breeze. Chamber pots were under each bed, as the outside lavatory was in the enclosed yard, near the washhouse and the coalhouse. In this chilly, windowless, outdoor building there was a long, well-scrubbed, wooden seat, with two circular holes, each of which was fitted with a lift-off wooden lid. It was the job of the men-folk of the household to empty this facility and it was a time when we two children were told to keep clear, as it wasn't the pleasantest of tasks, either to perform, or to witness.

Barry and Norma Seaton on the steps of the farmhouse at Whitfield Brow, possibly 1939

Barry and I were enrolled at the local school at Bridge End, Frosterley. It was here that my grandfather and his siblings had been taught. It would have been quite unchanged since their day, both in the style of teaching, and in the classrooms, one of which had a large, open fire surrounded by a huge fireguard. I wasn't given proper lessons at school, as we weren't expected to stay long, so I spent many hours copying out letters of the alphabet in 'copperplate' handwriting, using an old-fashioned pen, and ink. Our mother herself had chosen our wartime evacuee destination. Had we not been there, John and Lizzie would probably have had other children, or even a family 'billeted' upon them, as, for most of the war years, the two of them were occupying quite a big house, on their own. Because she wasn't tied by restrictions, Mother was free to take us home, whenever she chose. Besides, the winter weather would have made it difficult for us 'townies' to get back and forth to school, a two-mile walk over Hill End that we had to make on our own and we were very young. The road might have had a tarmac surface by the time we lived there, but it was just as steep as it had always been and the two of us, as young, unaccompanied children, had no sense of time or urgency and we were easily distracted and slowed down. I remember, one day, standing over a moving molehill, at the side of the road, waiting for the little, burrowing mole to appear, which he did. This was a new experience for us and we probably stood there for quite a long time. All of our memories, of course, were childhood memories, and we were protected from the anxieties suffered by the older generation. We were well fed and we were allowed to taste the warm, frothy milk, straight from the cow. Every day we had delicious homemade white bread, homemade butter and homemade jam and, when we weren't supervised, which seemed to be most of the time, we went into the dairy and helped ourselves to animal feed, which was kept there in large bins. We brought in the five cows from the field, we helped with haymaking, we collected eggs, fed the calves and played freely, exploring together the fresh smelling moorland and the nearby woods and stream.

Ninth Generation

During the war, John and Lizzie's daughter, Mary, my mother's cousin, went to Newcastle to take up nursing. She later married John Charters and had a son, Alan. Albert, Mary's younger brother, who was born on 21st November 1922, joined the army. He had worked on the farm as a youth and farming was a 'reserved occupation' during the war, but John and Lizzie could obviously manage alone. When he was called up he was a 'kiln hand' and lorry driver and in the summer of 1944 he married Margaret Furnace, a local girl. In his army release book, dated 15th January 1948 he was designated as an Amphibian Training Wing Instructor and he was given first class references. John and Lizzie left the farm and retired to rent a house in Stanhope, where John died. He was buried in Frosterley. Lizzie had a long retirement and she continued to live on in Stanhope, in a house in the High Street, before moving to Newcastle to live with her daughter, Mary. She died when she was in her eighties and her ashes were returned to Frosterley, where they were buried.

For a time Albert and Margaret lived in semi-detached, wartime housing called 'brown houses' which were built between Hill End and Frosterley.

When he left the army, Albert took up a job as a driver with a company called Corbets and lived for a while in Stanhope. He later moved to Frosterley, where he and Margaret brought up their three children. Albert Leslie Thompson was born in 1947, Lynn Elizabeth in 1953 and Gillian Margaret in 1956. We could have expected that Albert's life, free from the hard labour and bad working conditions of either the lead mines, or the limestone quarries, would have been longer than that of most of his male forebears, but he suffered a heart attack outside his house on his way to work and died, suddenly, at the age of 61. His wife, Margaret, didn't survive him for very long and they are now buried, together, in Stanhope cemetery.

Thus, the Thompson's lead mining past in Teesdale and Weardale came to an end. The lead mines may have lost their hold on the lives of the population, but they have left their mark, both on the people themselves and on the landscape, which was altered forever by the mine workings. Between the road to Frosterley and the houses at Whitfield Brow, the landscape is recovering. The hillside is covered in long grass and bracken, but very little vegetation grows on the disturbed earth of the spoil heaps, which are higher up the hill, nearer the two rows of houses. Mother Nature has tried her best and has hidden them in a thin coating of smooth grass, which is often dug through by rabbits to expose the small rocks left behind after all the lead ore had been extracted from them. Only two small mining buildings remain, one of them semi-derelict, to remind us that this very rural, moorland scene was once a hive of industry. The many children who lived at Bollihope in the days when the lead mines were still in production witnessed daily scenes of men, horses and machinery, working in dust, noise and steam to extract lead from the rock brought down from the mine, but now all is reasonably quiet and rural. In the valley bottom, beside the river, there are still many bare humps and bumps in the landscape, which leave a clearer picture of what the area looked like when it was an industrial site that was both quarried and mined. Up at Whitfield Brow, the old farm buildings have been converted into 'new homes'. The miners' houses have lost their uniform identity of sash windows and plain, stout, seldom-used front doors, as most of them have now been modernised. The old mine was reopened in 1970 to prospect for fluorspar and the track up to it is now fenced off and gated.